D1737340

SCHOOL PRINCIPALS AND CHANGE

SOURCE BOOKS ON EDUCATION
(Vol. 33)

GARLAND REFERENCE LIBRARY
OF SOCIAL SCIENCE
(Vol. 783)

SCHOOL PRINCIPALS AND CHANGE

Michael D. Richardson
Paula M. Short
Robert L. Prickett

GARLAND PUBLISHING, INC. • NEW YORK & LONDON
1993

Library of Congress Cataloging–in–Publication Data

Richardson, Michael D. (Michael Dwight), 1949-
    School principals and change / by Michael D. Richardson, Paula M.
Short, Robert L. Prickett.
        p. cm. — (Garland reference library of social science ; vol. 783.
Source books on education ; vol. 33)
    Includes bibliographical references.
    ISBN 0–8153–0383–1 (alk. paper)
    1. School principals—United States. 2. Educational leadership—
United States. 3. School management and organization—United
States. I. Short, Paula M. II. Prickett, Robert L. III. Title.
IV. Series: Garland reference library of social science ; v. 783.
V. Series: Garland reference library of social science. Source books
on education ; vol. 33.
LB2831.92.R53 1993
371.2'012'0973—dc20   92–28436
                                                                    CIP

Printed on acid-free, 250-year-life paper
Manufactured in the United States of America

Contents

Preface

It has been said that the public school principal has one of the most difficult jobs in America, and who could argue? Public education is under fire like no other time in our history. The courts are making the principal's job a legal nightmare, and teachers are the largest collective bargaining group in the United States. Yet children are still in need of an education and somehow brave men and women continue to fill the principal ranks and take on the challenge—the challenge of making our schools better.

One of the major ironies of recent educational reforms involves the evolution of the principal's role in public schools. In earlier times, the principal was viewed as a teacher with limited knowledge of administration. Conversely, with today's myriad of educational reforms, the principal is perceived in exactly the opposite view, an administrative manager with limited knowledge of the technology of teaching. Yet most researchers expect the principal to be the instructional leader of the school in addition to providing the necessary administrative management functions. This expectation is directly related to recent developments in the evolution of the principalship, particularly effective schools research.

The role of the principal is as varied as the individual who occupies the position. The principal must deal with numerous factors which infringe on role clarification and expectations. Among these factors are role ambiguity, goal setting behaviors, leadership behaviors, individual initiative, management behaviors, instructional management, symbolic leadership, personal characteristics, and situational influences. All these are operationalized in goal clarification for individual principals.

There have been several recent calls for a differentiation between the ideal perceived and the actual perceived roles of the principal. This book cannot settle the principal role conflicts between instructional leadership, administrative management, and the myriad of other roles the principal must occupy. However, a synthesis of pertinent literature is presented for clarification of present practices and speculation about future methods for dealing with these role conflicts. Logically, quality principals must wear several hats with equal regularity if they are to be effective leaders and efficient managers.

While some researchers have dissected the principalship for a greater understanding of its complexity, ultimately, the parts must be reassembled to reflect the immense interrelationships inherent in this most difficult of occupations. To all those who diligently serve as principals, to all those who wish to become a principal, and to all those who have enriched our lives by their constant devotion to this profession, this book is gratefully dedicated.

Acknowledgments

We wish to acknowledge the contribution of Scott Thomson of the National Policy Board on Educational Administration and the work of the National Commission for the Principalship on which this work is based. Regardless of the contributors, the final responsibility for this work has to be ours.

Our special thanks to Brenda Stiteler for the numerous manuscript revisions which she graciously completed. Thanks also to Jim Moore for his research contributions. This book is dedicated to Leah and Rick.

SECTION ONE
INTRODUCTION

CHAPTER 1

Introduction

Today more than any other time in history, schools are under close scrutiny. In light of the movement toward educational reform and the push for excellence in public schools, many rapid changes are occurring. Changes in student achievement and curriculum, as a result of implementation of new programs and teacher accountability, are just a few of the alterations suggested (Snyder and Anderson, 1986). Studies measure everything and everyone in schools. Some studies find problems, some try to solve problems, and some even deny that there are any problems. Change does not always come easily. More often, it is difficult, but can be made easier when someone takes the lead. In education, that someone is the school principal. Most researchers agree that an effective school requires an effective principal who is a primary force in making a school work and change occur.

BACKGROUND

Today, education is in a state of flux. Reform movements, community partnerships groups, parent involvement groups, politicians, school administrators, teachers, students and others are striving to build some sense of order from the confused myriad of signals given to and sent by the American education system.

In its April 1983 final report, the National Commission on Excellence in Education determined that America's very survival was in doubt. The culprit for this devastating threat was, of course, the failure of the American education system. According to the Commission, this alarming trend of decline could be attributed to weakness of purpose, confusion of vision, underuse of talent, and a lack of leadership.

Once again a crisis caused Americans to re-examine some basic educational premises and practices. As a reaction to the report, education and educators have undergone a strict scrutinizing and, in many cases, have been found to be unacceptable.

This reconstituted emphasis on recovering our lost preeminence has created a climate for changing the face of American education. A major thrust in this battle to regain that which was lost has been occurring in the arena of leadership. Arvin C. Blome and Mary Ellen James (1985) discussed the rationale behind the reform movement's current emphasis on American educational leadership as follows:

> ". . . the present reform era has made the concept of positive school leadership even more imperative: outside demands and resources must be mediated and orchestrated into a sensible plan . . ." (p. 51)

It would seem to be sensible and reasonable to state that effective educational systems are managed by effective leaders. But what is an effective principal? What sets this person apart from a mediocre principal? What skills do principals use to develop and maintain an effective school?

In order to identify the effective principal, the characteristics of an effective school must first be identified. Most researchers include some or all of the following: 1) a principal who is an active leader, 2) a positive school climate, 3) teachers and administrators who have high expectations for students, faculty, and themselves, 4) parents who are involved in the educational process, 5) productive methods of evaluating the curriculum, 6) efficient methods of evaluating teacher performance, 7) consequential methods of developing and evaluating student growth, 8) a realistic philosophy of education and, 9) opportunities for shared decision-making.

The effective school is a purposeful organization whose members seek, through common effort, to achieve established goals. School systems are composed of people, and people will determine whether the system succeeds or stagnates, serves its clients effectively or squanders its limited resources. Therefore, people create an effective school—it does not happen without vision, dedication, and hard work.

The effective school is a complex organization. With regard to the preceding characteristics, the principal is the driving force behind each school. The principal cannot accomplish all the tasks independently but must possess the knowledge and leadership ability to get them done, often creatively, within the context of the organization. The principal must help group members feel comfortable and at ease, help articulate and define objectives, and cooperatively work toward the accomplishment of school objectives.

The principal is responsible for leading and managing the school. Being in charge of the school means being visible to students, staff, and the public. The principal cannot sit at a desk behind closed doors hoping that everything gets done. The school organization does not function in a vacuum, it must have a viable, visible, sustaining force. That force is the principal.

With the increased complexity of the principalship, it is ironic that relatively little is known about how principals are identified or ultimately selected. Three factors of society in general, and in education specifically, color the image of the principalship. First, the principal is currently viewed as the person "in the middle." The principal is perceived to be a true middle manager, being bombarded from above by superintendents and school boards, from below by teachers, and from both sides by parents, community, and students. Additionally, the continuing educational reform movement places much emphasis on the instructional leadership role of the principal which is a different role from that historically practiced by many administrators. Consequently, school boards and superintendents expect principals to implement administrative policy while teachers and students expect instructional leadership and a supportive climate. Add the conflict inherent in the collective bargaining process, and the principalship is not as attractive as once perceived.

Second, societal pressures dictate that more women and minorities be named to the principalship. Research indicates that women occupy approximately three percent of all the principalships while minorities make up a similar percentage (Peterson & Finn, 1985). Although many areas may not have significant minority populations, women are the majority of employees in most school districts, but typically occupy a minority of the administrative positions.

Third, approximately fifty percent of all currently employed principals are age fifty-five (55) or over. Consequently, the most dramatic administrative turnover in educational history will occur during the next decade because of retirements. With the anticipation of such dramatic changes, school districts are encouraged to develop appropriate techniques for the selection of the next generation of principals.

HISTORY OF THE PRINCIPALSHIP

The Seventh Yearbook of the Department of Elementary School Principals traces the development of the school principalship through five stages: the one teacher, the head school teacher, the teaching principal, the building principal, and the supervising principal. The duties of the first three are largely teaching; those of the fourth, administration; and those of the fifth, supervision.

The title of principal of an elementary school was first used in New York and Buffalo about the middle of the 19th century. These early principals were little more than head teachers and assumed few administrative duties. Principals became important with the rapid increase in school enrollment which made necessary large elementary school buildings. Such expansion also increased the managerial and supervisory work in the school.

The secondary school principal is an outgrowth of the master of the Latin Grammar Schools and the academy. The modern high school principalship was developed during the period from about 1820 to 1860, and roughly paralleled the establishment of the superintendency. The superintendent of schools often took charge of the secondary schools, and in many cases served as principal. As the secondary schools grew and developed, the principalship emerged as a distinct position apart from the superintendency. Historically, the secondary school principal assumed more administrative responsibility and devoted less time to teaching. The principal also assumed major supervisory responsibilities for the school.

Today principals usually are selected by the superintendent of schools and appointed by the board of education. In addition to their educational and personal qualifications, principals typically have had experience as teachers.

ROLE OF THE PRINCIPAL

Historically, the role of the principal has taken many forms. The first principals were called "head teachers," who, although in charge of the school, spent most of their time in instructional programs teaching. The increasingly complex organizational demands of schools forced many principals to abandon instructional duties for management functions. To be successful today, principals have gone full circle back to being the instructional leader.

With so many demands on their time and talents, a special effort is required of principals who wish to earn the status of "instructional leader." The rewards are well worth the effort. The single most consistent finding of effective school research indicates that effective schools have principals who are instructional leaders. In William L. Rutherford's (1985) review of earlier research, he found that principals are effective leaders when they share five essential qualities.

> Effective principals: 1) have clear, informed visions of what they want their schools to become—visions that focus on students and their needs; 2) translate these visions into goals for their schools and expectations for the teachers, students, and administrators; 3) establish school climates that support progress toward these goals and expectations; 4) continuously monitor progress; and 5) intervene in a supportive or corrective manner when this seems necessary. (p. 32)

SKILLS

Possession of leadership skills and a strong knowledge base alone do not make a great school leader. There are various kinds of leaders. Some leaders are more successful than others and the qualities that make them productive are important to the organizational concept of effective schools. In recent years, the task of defining leadership has drawn considerable interest. Luvern L. Cunningham notes there are 350 definitions of leadership recorded in educational literature. Cunningham (1985) further states, "Leadership is whatever people believe it to be" (p. 17). Along that same line, John Naisbitt, author of *Megatrends* (1984), states, "The new leader is a facilitator, not an order giver" (p. 209). The traditional view of the leader as the absolute, unquestioned authority is slowly giving way to other less threatening styles of leadership.

As education changes, views of leadership change. Change has made leadership difficult to define. Robert W. Cole, editor *Phi Delta Kappan* (1985), offered these observations about leadership.

> And after all, what is a leader? Someone who articulates a vision and sets a course that others end up following. Effective principals, for example, seem to have a clear vision of what they want their schools to become—a vision that focuses on students and their needs—and they establish a climate that nurtures this vision. People have to want to follow a leader; compulsion is not leadership. That kind of top-down thinking has done enough damage.

Teaching and inspiring are an essential part of
leadership. The most effective leaders in any field lead
by educating their followers. (p. 2)

Cole's observations on leadership are a far cry from the authoritarian
masters of the past. It would seem that today's leaders are those
individuals who are capable of influencing others and capable of
facilitating the actions of those who willingly follow them. It would
seem that influencing others requires individuals to possess accurate
knowledge of themselves.

Ron Daughtery (1987) suggests that leaders share the same
characteristics as Maslow's self-actualized individual. According to
Daughtery, leaders share many of the following qualities: "intelligence,
verbal facility, sociability, initiative, originality, enthusiasm, confidence,
adaptability, popularity, and probably good looks" (p. 35).

Leaders need to possess the ability to influence and facilitate actions
and teach others by example. Leaders also seem to be those who are well
versed in the knowledge of themselves as well as those who follow them.
According to Roberds-Baxter (1986):

Good school administrators get things done; and
much of their success lies in being able to assess the
strengths of their staffs, assign tasks, appoint
committees, and relate to teachers that enhance their
potential and motivate them to work toward common
goals.

An ingredient essential to all of it is understanding
the fundamental differences in people. These differences
often can be identified by specific behaviors and the
people categorized by type. (p. 7)

Leadership is obviously a blending of many of the characteristics
previously listed. This list is hardly conclusive. Cunningham (1985)
suggests seven skills that should be acquired by an prospective leader. The
first of these is "focusing on the present and the future simultaneously"
(p. 18). Cunningham suggests that the prospective leader can accomplish
this first task through the development of the following abilities:

- the capacity to distinguish between and among
those things that require short-, medium-, and long-
range planning or attention;

- the ability to sense rates of change and the amount of lead time required to plan, anticipate, or otherwise respond to change;

- the practical art of focusing followers' attention on the future long enough so they arrive at a shared sense of what the future portends, before retreating to the temporary comfort of thinking only of the present;

- a rational framework for thinking and planning that is both comprehensive and simple enough to be practical;

- a certain toughness with regard to the task that must be done and an unwavering commitment to the task and its importance;

- the ability to work back from agreed-on institutional goals and objectives in order to cover all the steps that are necessary to achieve those objectives; and

- the ability to lead in emotionally charged situations. (p. 19)

The second skill necessary is "bridging the gaps between different interest groups" (p 19). According to Cunningham (1985),

This ability has two dimensions. The first dimension, essentially an internal one, involves communication and interaction with individuals and groups that have a stake in the everyday operations of the schools, e.g. students, parents, teachers, school board members, administrators, and other school employees. The second dimension, essentially external to the schools, involves relations with individuals, groups, organizations, and institutions in the community. (p. 19)

The third ability is "scanning, monitoring, and interpreting events" (p. 19). This ability requires the leader to develop an "efficient information-gathering technique, as well as some degree of personal and institutional discipline" (p. 19).

The fourth ability is "appraisal skill." Cunningham states:

Skill in appraisal is a crucial ingredient of effective leadership. The process of appraisal requires a leader to step back from or rise above the welter of everyday

events to pass judgment on a range of matters,
including self-estimates of his or her own performance.
(p. 19)

The fifth ability is "intuition." This process requires leaders to
"rely on their own unique but limited human capacity to process
information" (p. 19).

Cunningham's (1985) sixth desirable ability is "managing
symbols" (p. 20). This ability is a two-fold one. The first aspect is:

flow of images that surround individuals and
institutions. Over time, these images create
impressions, and taken in the aggregate, become the
basis for appraisal or judgments of the person or
institution.
There is a second aspect of symbolism worth
noting. Leaders are expected to participate in public
events of importance to their constituencies. (p. 20)

The last ability Cunningham (1985) identifies is "the leader as
teacher" (p. 20). Cunningham suggests that current literature finds that a
leader knows

the mission, the goals, and objectives of an enterprise
and teaches them continuously. The leader's behavior is
imitated by others in the institution or organization.
The extent to which others carry out the mission of the
institution or organization is linked to the leader's
success as a teacher. (p 20)

If these are the qualities a leader or a prospective leader possesses, and
these qualities can be acquired, then effective leadership may be able to
reverse the trend toward failure of American education.

Today's principal must have several qualities to run an effective
school: 1) the ability to envision, 2) human relations skills, including
group process skills, 3) a sense of purpose, urgency, or mission, 4) a
broad knowledge base, and 5) integrity and honesty. An effective principal
must have a vision of what the school should become and how the school
relates to the larger organizational scheme of district, community and
beyond.

Principals must have a plan for their staff to work toward. The
effective principal must also have a knowledge base firmly grounded in
learning, teaching, group process, and organizing people. Also, they must

have skills to help groups work toward common goals and a shared vision for schools. These items must then be combined with a very strong commitment to assist staff and students to improve schooling. The effective principal must also have a personal sense of mission. This mission must be communicated continuously to the staff, students, and parents in a variety of forms.

FUNCTIONS

Principals cannot allow the press for testing to overshadow the necessity for good human and public relations (Shoemaker & Fraser, 1981). We must remember that the school is there for the children. Principals must keep this in mind and work to improve human relations in their schools and communities. Principals must be enablers and help teachers to concentrate on teaching. Teachers must do the same and allow students to concentrate on learning.

Effective principals establish a climate in which the staff have a high level of satisfaction with their work. They also encourage a strong sense of participation and control over important educational decisions and activities in school. Effective principals accomplish this by: 1) using a participatory style of leadership, 2) exhibiting an open, professional, and collegial style that fosters joint discussion, evaluation, and improvement, and 3) working with others toward the perspectives and incentives of those he or she would persuade (Duttweiler & Hord, 1989).

The effective principal goes out of the way to help teachers solve problems; looks out for the personal welfare of teachers by staying after school to help with extra work, and provides necessary services (Duttweiler & Hord, 1989). Effective principals show concern for students. Although they cannot possibly be there for every student, they can instill this helping spirit. There must be a spirit of cooperation to bring out the best in a student body and a teaching staff (Sashkin, 1988).

Effective communication is essential for any leader and the school principal is no exception. Communication must be between groups and individuals. The principal must be able to communicate in a variety of ways. There are basically three different forms of communication: oral language, written language, and nonverbal language (Oliva, 1984). A principal does not have to be a great speaker to be successful but must be able to verbally communicate to different groups. A principal should use different forms of communication when talking to a group of college students and a group of students who skipped school. A principal must also be able to verbally treat people with respect. This greatly affects the quality of work that the combined effort will produce. Teachers also enjoy working for a principal who will verbally support them when they are wrong (Weller, 1985).

Nonverbal communication is something that takes place all the time. The facial and body gestures of an individual tell a big story. A smile, a frown, a grimace, and laughter can often convey a meaningful message. Principals should be able to read nonverbal gestures, while at the same time express similar gestures (Oliva, 1984).

SUMMARY

Honesty is a big key in dealing with people. Honesty can be very blunt sometimes, but people in the long run can respect and appreciate honesty. It has been found that high-performing principals have the ability to persuade or influence others through a number of means: gaining and sustaining attention and interest in group situations, using information or arguments, modeling the behaviors expected, or being direct in specifying what others will do. The principal is also sensitive to the ideas and opinions of others but behaves to ensure an understanding of the feelings and verbalizations of others (Duttweiler & Hord, 1989).

Studies show the effective school has a principal who has high expectations for the performance of teachers and students. School staff and administration must convey high expectations to students. People want to work in a situation where they know what to expect. Effective principals earn the respect of their teachers, students, and community and can bring about change.

CONCLUSION

In conclusion, effective schools have principals who share a great vision for the school with the faculty and have a definite plan to reach that vision. Effective leaders understand people and are good managers. Principals who demonstrate the variety of the skills and strategies discussed will have the greatest opportunity to develop effective schools. Effective leaders perform in such a manner as to enhance the school's culture. On the other hand, poor leaders allow the school's culture to fall into disarray.

Effective principals have diverse qualities which may sometimes contradict one another. This explains partly their flexibility and how they can deal with so many people and be successful. They can communicate to a variety of groups and individuals. Effective principals see that things are done right and ensure that they are doing the right things (Bennis, 1989).

NOTES

Bennis, W. (1989). *Why leaders can't lead.* San Francisco: Jossey-Bass.

Blome, A.C., & James, M.E. (1985). The principal as instructional leader: An evolving role. *NASSP Bulletin, 69* (485), 51.

Cole, R.W. (1985). The editor's page: Making chicken pie. *Phi Delta Kappan, 67* (1), 2.

Cunningham, L.L. (1985). Leaders and leadership: 1985 and beyond. *Phi Delta Kappan, 67* (1), 2.

Daughtery, R. (1987). A new look at leadership. *Thrust for Educational Leadership, 16* (4), 35.

Duttweiler, F.C., & Hord, S. (1989). *Dimensions of effective leadership.* Austin, TX: BEDL.

Naisbitt, J. (1984). *Megatrends.* New York, NY: Warner Books.

Oliva, P.F. (1984). *Supervision for today's schools.* New York: Longman.

Peterson, K.D., & Finn, C. (1985). Principals, superintendents, and the administrator's art. *The Public Interest, 79,* 127-131.

Rutherford, W.L. (1985). School principals as effective leaders. *Phi Delta Kappan, 67* (1), 32.

Sashkin, M. (1988). The visionary principal: School leadership for the next century. *Education and Urban Society, 20* (3), 239-249.1

Shoemaker, J., & Fraser, H.W. (1981, November). What principals can do: Some implications from studies of effective schooling. *Phi Delta Kappan, 63* (3), 178-182.

Snyder, K.J. & Anderson, R.H. (1986). *Managing productive schools: Toward an ecology.* Orlando, FL: Academic Press.

Weller, L.D. (1985). The principal: Catalyst for promoting effective schooling. *Action in Teacher Education, 7* (3), 7-12.

BIBLIOGRAPHY

1. Andrews, C. (1990). Evaluating principals: Research roundup. (ERIC Document Reproduction Service No. ED 318 131)

   Five recent studies included in this annotated bibliography highlight the diverse facets of an effective principal evaluation system. A technical report by Jerry W. Valentine and Michael L. Bowman includes a clinical instrument for assessing teachers' perception of principals' effectiveness. In a second report, Daniel L. Duke and Richard J. Stiggins give voice to pleas from principals that their chronic isolation from the central office be remedied by the institution of channels for ongoing communication. A report by Joseph Murphy and others examines the process of principal supervision and evaluation used by twelve California school districts whose student achievement scores are consistently excellent. A study by William C. Harrison and Kent D. Peterson examines the contrast between principals who were satisfied with their superintendents' handling of an evaluation procedure and those who were not. The final selection, a study by Mark E. Anderson, assimilates the lessons of previous research to lay out a strategy for principal evaluation that balances accountability with the nurturing of professional development. The study also contains detailed descriptions of systems used by two highly regarded Oregon school districts to evaluate their principals, and offers recommendations for other interested districts.

2. Bredeson, P.V. (1989). Empowered teachers-empowered principals: Principals' perceptions of leadership in schools. (ERIC Document Reproduction Service No. ED 311 598)

   As teachers assume a variety of leadership functions traditionally held by the principal and as they become much more of a self-managing professional work group, it is important to examine the implications of these changes for the leadership behavior of professionals credentialed as building principals. This paper presents data from in-depth structured interviews with ten principals (five elementary and five secondary) from two school districts (Centremont and Hillview, Pennsylvania). The school principals' leadership roles in teacher-empowered schools are identified and described. Findings define empowerment and address changes in the traditional leadership behaviors that support empowered teachers. The experiences with teacher empowerment in these two districts suggest that a clear definition of empowerment is less important than is a commitment to systematically engage teachers in decisions that affect their professional worklives in schools. (Seven references)

3. Cline, H.D., & Richardson, M.D. (1988). The reform of school administrator preparation: The Kentucky Principal's Internship Model. (ERIC Document Reproduction Service No. ED 315 871)

In response to the growing need for highly competent school administrators, Kentucky has mandated an administrator preparation program to reflect recommendations specified by the University Council for Educational Administration and reforms advocated by other national organizations. Designed to provide prospective principals with an appropriate knowledge base, the Kentucky Assembly's set of 1988 guidelines requires three years' teaching experience, a master's degree, and a minimum of eighteen semester hours of coursework in eight major areas. Candidates are required to complete an internship or employment as a practicing principal. After completing a certification program at the university, a candidate is issued a permit for the internship. During the internship, the candidate is monitored by the local school district and the university and given temporary certification for one year to complete the internship. Unsuccessful candidates are given another chance, if school districts are willing to hire them as principals. Successful completion entitles the candidate to certification for an additional four years. During this time, supplemental coursework must be completed. The primary focus of the internship program involves the opportunity for supervised practice and the framework for demonstration of competence. The program provides prospective principals with employment opportunities, allows closer coordination between school districts and universities, and establishes a network benefitting all parties.

4. Clouse, R.W. (1989). A Review of Educational Role Theory: A Teaching Guide for Administrative Theory. (ERIC Document Reproduction Service No. ED 314 824)

This document examines role theory in major studies related to educational administration. The nature and history of role theory are reviewed and three theoretical approaches to the study of role theory are described: (1) role conflict resolution theory; (2) role theory related to social systems theory; and (3) the fundamental interpersonal relations orientation theory of interpersonal behavior. Conclusions are drawn by the author about the historical value of role theory.

5. Daresh, J.C., & Playko, M.A. (1990). Mentor programs: Focus on the beginning principal. (ERIC Document Reproduction Service No. EJ 414 841)

Certain characteristics qualify individuals to serve as mentor principals, including experience as practicing school administrators, demonstration of positive leadership qualities, ability to question beginning administrators appropriately, acceptance of alternative management methods, desire to promote exceptional performance, ability to model continuous learning principles, and awareness of a school system's political and social realities.

6. Ellis, T.I. (1986). The principal as instructional leader. (ERIC Document Reproduction Service No. ED 274 031)

Research has verified that schools are rarely effective unless the principal is a proficient instructional leader. This article summarizes five recent studies examining the practices and quantities comprising good instructional leadership. A Seattle study by Richard L. Andrews disclosed a statistical correlation between student gains in reading and mathematics and teachers' perceptions of their principal's effectiveness—especially in schools with many low-income students. Phillip Hallinger and Joseph Murphy found that a community's socioeconomic status heavily affected the behavior of effective instructional leaders and their choice of management style. In San Francisco, David C. Dwyer found that proficient instructional leaders act on personal beliefs and values, as well as perceptions of their schools' and communities' needs. In Texas, William Rutherford and his associates studied the principal's impact on teachers' instructional improvement efforts. The most successful principals clearly communicated expectations, provided technical assistance, and monitored the results. Finally, Thomas Bird and Judith Warren Little showed that effective instructional leadership means cultivating and sustaining norms of civility, collegiality, and continuous improvement. A summary of each study is provided, together with full bibliographical and availability information.

7. Gunn, J.A., & Holdaway, E.A. (1986). Perceptions of effectiveness, influence, and satisfaction of senior high school principals. (ERIC Document Reproduction Service No. EJ 338 761)

A 1983-1984 Alberta study examined the job satisfaction of senior high school principals and its relationship to these principals' perceptions of their influence, their effectiveness, and their school's effectiveness. The selected indicators and best predictors of these variables, and associations with demographic variables, also were identified. (37 references)

8. Hallinger, P., & Murphy, J. (1985). Assessing the instructional management behavior of principals. (ERIC Document Reproduction Service No. EJ 328 595)

Presents results from a study examining the instructional management behavior of ten elementary school principals in a single school district. Discusses the development of an assessment method for this behavior, findings of principals' curriculum and instructional management, and tentative findings regarding personal and organizational factors associated with instructional management.

9. Hallinger, P., & Murphy, J. (1986). Instructional leadership in effective schools. (ERIC Document Reproduction Service No. ED 309 535)

The focus of this document is on the re-emergence of the principal as the school's instructional leader as attributable to effective schools research. The document presents a framework that conceptualizes instructional leadership as a two-dimensional construct comprised of leadership functions and leadership processes. The leadership functions described include: 1) framing and communicating school goals; 2) supervising and evaluating instruction; 3) coordinating curriculum; 4) developing high academic standards and expectations; 5) monitoring student progress; 6) promoting the professional development of teachers; 7) protecting instructional time; and 8) developing incentives for students and teachers. The leadership processes described are: communication, decision making, conflict management, group process, change process, and environmental interaction. (Eight references)

10. Hallinger, P., & Murphy, J. (1987). Organizational and social context and the instructional leadership role of the school principal. (ERIC Document Reproduction Service No. ED 309 528)

This article discusses the research concerning the relationship between the organizational and social context of schools and principal instructional leadership. The discussion centers on several contextual variables that include school level, staff composition, technical clarity and complexity, and district context. Particular attention is focused on the ways in which the social context of schools influences the principal's leadership role. Findings support the notions that the nature of the school's technology, the type of district support, the characteristics of the teaching staff, the school level, and the social context combine to form a school culture all of which creates a context for principal action, and more specifically, an approximate style of instructional leadership.

11. Hallinger, P., & Wimpelberg, R. (1989). New settings and changing paradigms for principal preparation. (ERIC Document Reproduction Service No. ED 308 579)

This paper adapts the framework developed by J. Murphy and P. Hallinger (1987) in a conceptual analysis of current approaches to educational leadership development. Murphy and Hallinger identified differentiating patterns of program operation in the areas of program content, program process, program focus, and what is referred to as "supporting tissue." The first section presents the conceptual framework. Next, examples from specific principal development programs are used to illustrate the range of variation among emerging approaches within the context of the conceptual framework. In the final section, the implications of the analysis for the future of principal training and development are discussed. (42 references)

12. Hampel, J. (1987). *Women Administrators: Networking for success. NASSP Bulletin, 71* (501), 44–46.

In this article the author presents a historical perspective of women's role in educational administration. Hampel points out that in 1928 eighteen percent of secondary principalships were filled by women, while in 1972 only 1.7 percent of secondary principals were female. The author speculates that networking has the most potential for helping women succeed in educational administration.

13. Hoyle, J.R. (1991). The principal and the pear tree. (ERIC Document Reproduction Service No. EJ 425 551)

School principals are in a difficult environment filled with stress and plagued by weak support. Most principals are unprepared for site-based decision making. University professors must take the initiative to use the emerging knowledge base and develop professional studies degree and staff development programs to prepare principals. (24 references)

14. Johnson, N.A., & Holdaway, E.A. (1990). School effectiveness and principals' effectiveness and job satisfaction: A comparison of three school levels. (ERIC Document Reproduction Service No. EJ 418 923)

Parallel studies in Alberta elementary, junior high, and senior high schools found school-level differences in principal's opinions about specific facets of their school's effectiveness, their own effectiveness, and their own job satisfaction. Teachers and superintendents rated school and principal effectiveness lower than did principals. (56 references)

15. Lotto, L.S., & Murphy, J. (1988). Making sense of schools as organizations: Cognition and sensemaking in schools. (ERIC Document Reproduction Service No. ED 304 749)

After a review of the literature on cognitive "cause maps" in organizational decision-making, this study describes a midwestern elementary school from the perspective of individual sensemaking, captured through individual cognitive maps of cause-effect relationships.

Data was collected with an adaptation of Bougon's (1983) Self-Q interviewing technique, in which respondents first ask themselves questions, then verify key concepts drawn from the questions, and finally indicate the causal relationships among the most important concepts and the nature of those relationships. Creating the individual cause maps involved moving from a broad, holistic assessment of the cause map to the delineation of subparts. At each stage, causal findings were interpreted against the substantive content of the concepts evoked by the individual respondent. Examples are drawn from four individual case studies of first-grade teachers, and findings are summarized with regard to the nature of the concepts used by the teachers, their perceived level of influence, the utility of examining the causal structure of individual maps, and the systematic structural differences across individuals on some critical dimensions not fully examined to date. Appended are tables of key concepts with the teachers' definitions, references, and individual case studies of the four teachers.

16. Lyman, L. (1987). Hey, Central Office: Here's how to help principals. (ERIC Document Reproduction Service No. EJ 350 666)
    Presents suggestions for superintendents and central office executives to provide support for principals. Principals can be helped in the following ways: hire the best principals, look within the system for principal candidates, provide training in instructional leadership, inform principals about legal matters, and visit principals often.

17. Murphy, J., et al. (1987). The administrative control of principals in effective school districts. (ERIC Document Reproduction Service No. EJ 371 957)
    Investigates the nature of administrative control in twelve instructionally effective school districts in California. Nine control functions are assumed to affect student outcomes by influencing curriculum and instruction. Findings from interviews with superintendents revealed more district-level control of principal behavior and site activity than anticipated.

18. Murphy, J., et al. (1985). Supervising and evaluating principals: Lessons from effective districts. (ERIC Document Reproduction Service No. EJ 327 943)
    A recent study indicates that the superintendent's personal involvement in principal supervision and evaluation, including frequent school visits, can be a key ingredient in school effectiveness.

19. Ortiz, F.I. (1988). Theorizing about the principalship. (ERIC Document Reproduction Service No. ED 298 621)

Several recent articles theorizing about the principalship are compared, contrasted, and analyzed with focus on leadership and changing roles. One main difficulty found in the first article—a literature review (Murphy)—was the absence of clarity of definitions among researchers. Several common issues emerged, including a causal relationship between administrative leadership and organizational outcomes, the logistical support for educational innovation, an establishment of the relationship between interpersonal orientation and perceptions of role clarity, and an examination of the structural-functionalist tradition. The conclusions are based on the lack of disciplined research based on one theoretical model. Suggestions are given for further research as to placement of the principal and the school site within the school district, and the application of the power and conflict model regarding the principalship.

20. Richardson, M.D., et al. (1987). How can principals implement Tennessee's Instructional Model (TIM)? 3 C's to constructive change. (ERIC Document Reproduction Service No. ED 286 260)

A model is presented which helps principals plan and evaluate instructional improvement. Described in relation to educational reform in Tennessee, the model assigns to principals the responsibility of implementing the instructional changes required by a career ladder program. Research shows that continuing education, communication, and climate (the three "C's") are desirable in organizational change. The change process is founded on six concepts that build upon one another in the form of a pyramid: 1) human relations, 2) knowledge, 3) expectations, 4) feedback, 5) patience, and 6) reward. To better human relations, principals should first build the foundation for change through interactions that motivate teachers to cooperate. A principal's attitude and interactions create the needed climate of trust and cooperation. Understanding a model and the ability to demonstrate its concepts are necessary to assist teachers in skill improvement and increase in knowledge. Teachers must feel that the principal expects them to do well. Principals should convey a positive sense of accomplishment to the teacher; high expectations bring effective implementation of changes. Feedback is essential for teachers to know how well they are doing and what is expected of them. If principals spend sufficient time in conference and in classroom observation, teachers will perceive that the process and their learning of it are supported. Near the pyramid's pinnacle, patience requires that principals work individually with each teacher and assess progress. Principals will similarly want teachers' patience with their own attempts to fill the instructional leadership role. Two rewards are the apex of the pyramid. Giving an extrinsic reward for improvement helps teachers through difficult times and improvement itself provides the intrinsic reward. Reward completes the climb to constructive change. Twelve references are appended.

21. Richardson, M.D. (1988). The Administrative Assessment Center: An opportunity for service. (ERIC Document Reproduction Service No. ED 301 930)

In 1988, the Department of Educational Leadership at Western Kentucky University (WKU) established the Western Kentucky Assessment Center, sponsored by the National Association of Secondary School Principals (NASSP). This document provides an overview of the history and methods of NASSP assessment centers, followed by a discussion of costs to participating districts. Participation is recommended for districts because of the need for objective data regarding potential administrators, and the participation of practicing principals in developmental activities is identified as a critical component. The paper concludes with a brief discussion of the success of assessment centers elsewhere.

22. Richardson, M.D., et al. (1989). Changing principal preparation programs: A five-phase model. (ERIC Document Reproduction Service No. ED 313 790)

The necessity for training highly competent individuals to assume educational leadership positions will be critical in the near future, since a sizeable percentage of school administrators and professors of educational administration will retire over the next decade. The programs preparing current administrators are not equipped to meet the demands of twenty-first century schools. This paper describes an initial attempt to reform principal preparation programs using a five-step process. Administrator preparation requirements outlined by the National Commission on Excellence in Educational Administration in 1987 include five strands: 1) the study of administration; 2) the study of educational administration's technical core; 3) application of research findings and methods to problems; 4) supervised practice; and 5) demonstration of competence. The American Association of School Administrators has developed guidelines featuring the most critical goals, competencies, and delivery components for inclusion in administrator preparation programs. The National Association of Secondary School Principals has also identified twelve important skill areas. In 1987, the Kentucky State Department of Education mandated that educational administration programs in the state provide knowledge in 11 areas and directed reforms initiated at Western Kentucky University. The Department of Educational Leadership received a Danforth Foundation grant to further exemplary and innovative administrator preparation programs. The program's five stages are program admission, formal course work, testing, the opportunity for supervised practice and demonstration of competence, and mentoring. Included is a list of seventeen references.

23. Richardson, M.D., et al. (1989). A descriptive analysis of Kentucky elementary school principals. (ERIC Document Reproduction Service No. ED 311 557)

America is experiencing renewed interest in the important role school administrators play in initiating and sustaining school excellence. The perception of the school principal as a passive, reactive manager has yielded to a more accurate recognition of the administrator as a proactive instructional leader. To obtain relevant information concerning the demographics of practicing Kentucky elementary principals and the role they play in educational quality and reform, a total of 1,122 questionnaires were mailed to both public and private school principals in the state. The initial mailing took place in September 1988, with a follow-up in October 1988; the usable response rate was 50.8 percent. The most obvious conclusions from an analysis of the data were that Kentucky elementary principals were white, middle-aged men with an average salary approximately 75 percent higher than teachers. The majority had slightly more than ten years total experience as a principal, but over 60 percent plan to retire within the next ten years. Most were principals of small schools who worked over 50 hours per week. Further, most were satisfied with the quality of their inservice training and the current state administrative certification requirements.

24. Richardson, M.D., & Prickett, R.L. (1991). A comprehensive evaluation of Kentucky's beginning principal intern program. (ERIC Document Reproduction Service No. ED 331 159)

In 1985 the Kentucky General Assembly passed a comprehensive educational reform package including provisions for the Kentucky Beginning Principal's Intern Program (KBPIP). Evaluating the KBPIP involved three phases: identification of research goals, objectives, and data collection instruments; collection of data from participants; and dissemination of data and results. Thirty-six first-year intern principals were interviewed to gather data regarding the intern principal, the strengths and weaknesses of the committee structure, and the program's impact on the intern principal, as well as to develop comparative data for future planning. Preliminary findings indicate that the KBPIP is a successful program as perceived by both intern principals and committee members. Recommendations include mandatory training sessions for committee members and required internships for all new principals and assistant principals. Forty-two tables delineate demographic variables of respondents and their answers to survey questions.

25. Stocklinski, J., & Miller-Colbert, J. (1991). The Comer Process: Moving from "I" to "We." (ERIC Document Reproduction Service No. EJ 419 920)

The Comer Process is a research-based school improvement model stressing collaboration, consensus, and communication for problem solving in academic, social, and staff development areas. The process allows school staff and parents to work together and to decide what is in the best interest of children.

CHAPTER 2

Reform and the Principalship

INTRODUCTION

Since the early 1980s, there has been a growing emphasis on restructuring American public education (Cuban, 1990; Chubb and Moe, 1990; Frymier, 1987; Maeroff, 1988). The focus of restructuring has stemmed from the recognition that the world is rapidly evolving both as a technological and global society (Hodgkinson, 1985). These societal changes affect how schools are to prepare students to be productive citizens in the twenty-first century (Toeffler, 1980).

Technological Advances

The world's knowledge base has doubled twice in this century and continues to increase geometrically (Cornish, 1986). Business and industry leaders forecast that current data processing and information systems will be replaced by "sophisticated devices for knowledge creation, capture, transfer, and use" (Dede, 1989, p. 23). Technology will restructure the tasks of the worker in the workplace requiring greater use of higher-order thinking skills (Dede, 1989).

Global Interdependence and Cultural Diversity

Futurists predict that global and multi-cultural pressures will alter the workplace creating an economy that is globally interdependent (Benjamin,

1989). This dictates the need for greater understanding and knowledge of world cultures and ability to cope with diversity of context.

Changes in the Workplace

Teams will increasingly become the way people work in all types of organizations. Studies of effective businesses suggest that the collective knowledge, skills, and creative energy of groups of individuals enhances the quality and quantity of output in organizations (Lawler, 1986).

Impact on Education

The changing society dictates that students will need skills and competency in critical thinking, reasoning, and creative problem solving (Dede, 1989). The team structure in the workplace demands that workers function in a cooperative setting, focusing on group task performance and collaborative learning (Dede, 1989). Schools must also function in environments that support critical thinking, collaboration, cooperative learning, and participant involvement in critical decision making (Jenkins, 1988; Lieberman & Miller, 1984; Greer & Short, 1990). In addition, some research indicates schools must restructure significantly in order to address student learning (David, Cohen, Honetschlager, & Traiman, 1990).

REFORM EFFORTS IN EDUCATION

Inherent in the restructuring theme are implications for school structure and school leadership. Many suggest that if schools are to address successfully the needs of students for the twenty-first century, then changes must occur not only in instruction but in the way schools are structured for decision making, collaboration among participants, and accountability (David et al., 1990). Commissions have recommended that schools be restructured to become flexible, autonomous units capable of solving problems at the school-base level (Thomson, 1990). The changing environment requires schools to maximize all human potential within the organization to better prepare students to live in an evolving society (Thomson, 1990).

Changes in the School Structure

Success in business and industry with the team approach for greater participant involvement in decision making has affected the restructuring of schools (Greer & Short, 1990). The creation of self-managing teams in business has been successful in empowering participants and improving the quality of the work of those companies (Hackman & Oldham, 1980; Lawler, 1986; Manz & Sims, 1987). Studies in participative decision making in business and industry have revealed that worker involvement in key decisions increases productivity, sense of ownership, and commitment (Lawler, 1986).

Traditionally, school-based participants have been excluded from key decisions that greatly affect their work design (Little, 1982; Zielinski, 1983). While administrators may seek information and advice in making decisions for the school, final decisions typically are made by administration. Teachers are believed to be unable or unwilling to accept the responsibility of decision making (English & Hill, 1990). However, the current restructuring movement recognizes the need to empower school participants as authority, and decision making is moved from the central office to school-based teams (David et al., 1990; *Principals for 21st Century Schools*, 1990). The major thrust in efforts to change the school structure includes (1) shared governance among school participants; (2) greater teacher opportunities for collaboration with control over their work environment and work condition; and (3) restructuring roles and responsibilities to create a sense of shared leadership in the school (Chubb & Moe, 1990; Cuban, 1990; Maeroff, 1988). Jenkins (1988) states that "to empower others is to give a stakeholder share in the movement and direction of the enterprise" (p. 149). Lightfoot (1986) defines empowerment as the opportunities that an individual has for responsibility, choice, autonomy, and authority.

Further changes revolve around communication. Communication in the traditional school reflects one-way, top down movement of information. Restructured schools support two-way, cross-team discussions on all issues of concern to school participants (English & Hill, 1990). Problems and issues may be identified by anyone in the school and decisions made with collaboration and involvement of all school participants (English & Hill, 1990; Short, Greer, & Michael, 1991). Many types of team structures build links among faculty, principal, and students (English & Hill, 1990; *Principals for 21st Century Schools*, 1990; Short et al., 1991). Site-based budgeting can involve all or teams of school-level participants in staffing and programmatic decisions (English & Hill, 1990).

Accountability in restructured schools moves from school effectiveness indicators—drop-out rates, attendance, standardized test scores—to learner effectiveness indicators—assessment of mastery skills with criterion-referenced tests, portfolios of student products indicating empowerment, creativity, and self-directed learning (Greer & Short, 1990; English & Hill, 1990).

REFORM EFFORTS IN SCHOOL LEADERSHIP

Changes in School Leadership

Primary in the restructuring movement is school-based management and decision-making (*Principals for 21st Century Schools*, 1990). In addition, restructured schools will be more collaborative with greater participant involvement in all aspects of school restructuring (Thomson, 1990; *Principals for 21st Century Schools*, 1990; Short et al., 1991). The restructured school will affect the role of the principal and dictate knowledge and skills that must be acquired to successfully provide leadership in changing schools (English & Hill, 1990; Thomson, 1990; *Principals for 21st Century Schools*, 1990).

To provide leadership required in the restructured school, individuals in the principalship must be change agents with skills in creating collaborative action (Thomson, 1990). The development and utilization of all human resources within the organization is the unique challenge of school leaders. The successful school leader must embrace innovation and risk taking as necessary for renewal and for meeting the ever-evolving needs of diverse students in the changing environment (*Principals for 21st Century Schools*, 1990).

Two national associations for school principals, the National Association of Secondary School Principals and the National Association of Elementary School Principals, have issued documents outlining specific skills and knowledge that principals in restructured schools will require (Thomson, 1990; *Principals for 21st Century Schools*, 1990). These skills closely relate to the changing context of schools.

The recommendations of the National Association of Elementary School Principals are based on a set of assumptions about the characteristics of restructured schools which include: (1) principals will be leading teachers who themselves will be exercising leadership in an environment of shared governance; (2) schools will increase their efforts to effectively prepare students for a global society and economy; (3) the elementary and middle school principalship will become more specialized; (4) principals will continue to exercise instructional leadership skills in order to provide the kinds of instructional experiences required by students; (5) school-based decision making and management will grow; (6) the building of a collaborative environment with participant involvement will require high levels of interpersonal skills for principals; (7) the development of the human resources in the organization will require principals to utilize adult learning theories; and (8) sweeping technological advances will affect the role of the principal, requiring continual professional development for principals (*Principals for 21st Century Schools*, 1990).

With the above assumptions undergirding the restructuring of the role of school principals, the National Association of Elementary Schools Principals has established a set of skills and competencies that characterize the new leader. These are as follows: (1) knowledge of effective instructional practices; (2) effective leadership skills; (3) skills in motivating and guiding teacher leaders; (4) knowledge of curriculum development; (5) knowledge of child development including children under five years of age; (6) effective communication skills for complex communication patterns; (7) effective interpersonal skills; (8) planning and implementation skills; (9) knowledge and understanding about the rapidly changing society; (10) knowledge of effective school practices; (11) knowledge of technological applications to management and instruction; (12) skills in effectively using the political process to achieve school goals; (13) skills in site-based management; (14) ability to build partnerships with parents and the school; (15) skills in gathering appropriate data for decision making; and (16) skills in developing a rich school climate and culture that is conducive to empowerment (*Principals for 21st Century Schools*, 1990).

Similarly, the National Commission for the Principalship, sponsored by the National Association of Secondary School Principals and the National Association of Elementary School Principals, indicates that the major role of principals in restructured schools is categorized by four domains (Thomson, 1990). Based on many of the assumptions espoused by the elementary principals' group, the focus is on two dimensions. One dimension relates to the exercise of broad leadership in developing the culture that supports collaboration and team involvement in decision making, innovation, and risk taking. The other dimension focuses on the functional aspects of leadership—those principal activities which ensure the tasks of the organization are accomplished (Thomson, 1990).

Specifically, the four categories of domains identified by the National Commission for the Principalship are (1) functional domains including leadership, problem analysis, judgment, delegation, implementation, information collection, and organizational oversight; (2) programmatic domains including curriculum design, student development, staff development, assessment, resource allocation, and instruction; (3) interpersonal domains including motivation, sensitivity, oral communication, and written communication; and (4) contextual domains including philosophical and cultural values, legal issues, policy and political influences, and public and media relations (Thomson, 1990).

It is evident from the work of these national organizations and other groups (Thomson, 1990; *Principals for 21st Century Schools*, 1990; Short et al., 1991) that the restructuring of public education has focused the role of the school leader squarely on facilitating the development of school organizations that engage participants in collaborative efforts and shared governance. In addition, restructuring calls for school leaders to function as change agents, having the skills to create a synergy toward organizational renewal and innovation. Finally, leaders in restructured schools must demonstrate skills in utilizing forces outside the school to help the school achieve its vision of quality instruction for students. If the role of the school leader is changing, how are preparation programs affected by the reform efforts in education?

Changes in Principal Preparation Programs

The call for reform of principal preparation programs can be seen as early as 1982 in Pitner's (1982) recommendations that educational leaders re-examine the training needs of university administrative preparation programs in terms of content, scope, delivery, and practice. Pitner (1982) recognized that traditional preparation programs must restructure to provide greater reality-oriented preparation with improved clinical experience. Educational leaders began to recognize that to build the kinds of skills needed by principals in restructured schools, university programs need to emphasize theoretical and clinical knowledge with greater collaboration by practitioners (Hoyle, English, & Steffy, 1985; Hoyle, English, & Steffy, 1990; *Improving the Preparation of School Administrators: An Agenda for Reform*, 1989). Systematic efforts to reform principal preparation programs began in 1987 with the publication of *Leaders for America's Schools*, the report of the National Commission for Excellence in Educational Administration (1987). The commission was formed through the efforts of the University Council for Educational Administration supported by foundations and a number of professional educational organizations. The report made several significant recommendations relative to preparation programs for school leaders. Specifically, the report recommended the following: administrator preparation programs be designed after the professional school model; programs for the recruitment and placement of ethnic minorities and women should be initiated by universities; public schools should become full partners in the preparation of school administrators; and professional development activities should be an integral component of the careers of professors and practitioners (*Leaders for America's Schools*, 1987). In addition, the Commission recommended that educational leadership be redefined, that the National Policy Board for Educational Administration be established, that preparation programs very small in size be eliminated, and that licensure programs be reformed (*Leaders for America's Schools*, 1987).

The report of the National Commission on Excellence in Educational Administration has forced professional preparation programs to address (1) clinical experiences of students; (2) the development of cohorts of students for the duration of coursework; (3) the role of practitioners in the preparation of school administrators; (4) the development of problem-solving, reflective skills of administrators; (5) the development of administrators who can facilitate the evolution of a professional organizational structure; (6) the development of collaborative models between the university and the public schools for school improvement purposes and research; and (7) the role of universities in the continual professional development of practicing administrators.

CONCLUSION

The call for reform of public education by the restructuring of schools and school leadership has greatly affected the role school principals will assume in these restructured schools. Principals will assume the role of facilitator, providing leadership in the development of a school climate supportive of shared governance, greater participant empowerment, and school-based decision making. In addition, school principals must be able to more effectively focus human resources on the development of student potential, empowering students to become self-directed, life-long learners (Short et al., 1991).

NOTES

Benjamin, S. (1989). An ideascape for education: What futurists recommend. *Educational Leadership, 47* (1), 8-12.

Chubb, J. & Moe, T. (1990). *Politics, markets, and America's schools.* Washington, DC: Brookings Institute.

Cornish, E. (1986). Educating children for the 21st century. *Curriculum Review, 25* (4), 12-17.

Cuban, L. (1990). Reforming again, again, and again. *Educational Researcher, 19* (1), 3-13.

David, J., Cohen, M., Honetschlager, D., & Traiman, S. (1990). *State Actions to Restructure Schools: First Steps.* Washington, DC: National Governors' Association.

Dede, C. (1989). The evolution of information technology: Implications for curriculum. *Educational Leadership, 47* (1), 23-26.

English, F.W. & Hill, J.C. (1989). *Restructuring: The Principal and Curriculum Change.* Reston, VA: The National Association of Secondary School Principals.

Frymier, J. (1987). Bureaucracy and the neutering of teachers. *Phi Delta Kappan, 69* (1), 9-14.

Greer, J. & Short, P. (1990). The Empowered School District Project. A grant report submitted to the Danforth Foundation.

Hackman, J.R. & Oldham, G.R. (1980). *Work redesign.* Reading, MA: Addison-Wesley.

Hodgkinson, H.L. (1985). *All one system.* Washington, DC: Institute for Educational Leadership.

Hoyle, J.R., English, F.W., & Steffy, B.E. (1986, 1990). *Skills for successful school leaders.* Arlington, VA: American Association of School Administrators.

Jenkins, K. (1988). Metaphor and mindset for educational leadership. *The Educational Forum, 52* (2), 143–151.

Lawler, E.E. (1986). *High-involvement management: Participative strategies for improving organizational performance.* San Francisco: Jossey-Bass.

Lieberman, A. & Miller, L. (1984). *Teachers, their world and their work: implications for school improvement.* Alexandria, VA: Association for Supervision and Curriculum Development.

Lightfoot, S.L. (1986). On goodness of schools: Themes of empowerment. *Peabody Journal of Education, 63* (30), 9–28.

Manz, C. C. & Sims, H. P., Jr. (1987). Leading workers to lead themselves: The external leadership of self-managing teams. *Administrative Science Quarterly, 32* (1), 106–128.

Maeroff, G.I. (1988). A blueprint for empowering teachers. *Phi Delta Kappan, 69* (71), 472–477.

National Association of Elementary School Principals. (1990). *Principals for 21st century schools.* Alexandria, VA: NAESP.

National Commission on Excellence in Educational Administration. (1987). *Leaders for America's schools.* The report of the Commission on Excellence in Educational Administration. Tempe, AZ: Arizona State University and the University Council for Educational Administration.

National Policy Board for Educational Administration. (1989). *Improving the preparation of school administrators.* Charlottesville, VA: University of Virginia.

Pitner, N. (1982). *Training of the school administrator: A state of the art.* An occasional paper from the Center for Educational Policy and Management. Eugene, OR: The University of Oregon.

Short, P.M., Greer, T.J., & Michael, R. (1991). Restructuring schools through empowerment: Facilitating the process. *Journal of School Leadership, 1* (2), 127–139.

Thomson, S. (1990). *Principals for our changing schools.* Report of the National Commission on the Principalship. Fairfax, VA: National Commission on the Principalship.

Toffler, A. (1980). *The third wave*. New York: Bantam Books.

Zielinski, A.E. & Hoy, W.L. (1983). Isolation and alienation in elementary school. *Educational Administration Quarterly, 19* (2), 27–45.

BIBLIOGRAPHY

26. Blumberg, A. (1989). *School administration as a craft*. Boston: Allyn and Bacon.

Blumberg uses the metaphor *craft* to provide an exciting view of the nature of administrative work. His use of the metaphor *art* focuses on the more implicit, tacit, and intuitive aspects of administrative work. The impact of the book is to view administration as reflective practice. Within this context, Blumberg specifies how administrators think about their work, the link between formal practice and on-the-job training, and if reflective practice can be taught.

27. David, J., Cohen, M., Honetschlager, D., & Traiman, S. (1990). *State actions to restructure schools: First steps*. Washington, DC: National Governors' Association.

This paperback book offers a brief discussion of current reform initiatives in five states. There is a concise presentation of the components of restructuring, including curriculum and instruction, authority and decision making, new staff roles, and accountability systems. The presentation of restructuring efforts in the five states is augmented by a discussion of how these states are approaching change and a prediction for the long-term impact of such efforts.

28. Donaldson, G. & Quaglia, R. (1989). Integrating knowledge in educational administration: Moving beyond context. In *Improving the Preparation of School Administrators, No. 3*. Charlottesville, VA: The National Policy Board for Educational Administration.

This chapter describes the development and implementation of an experiential course in educational administration designed to address the demands for competency-based preparation programs. Utilizing the case study method, the authors present the underlying conceptual framework that guided the development of the course. Feedback from students is presented.

29. Drake, T.L., & Roe, W.H. (1986). *The principalship*. New York: Macmillan.

This book, directed at the principalship in general, is based on the assumption that the primary role of the principal is to develop the human potential available among teachers in order to better provide for student learning. Principal leadership with teachers is central to any administrative activity in which the principal is involved. Thus, a major portion of the book focuses on how to organize schools to improve learning, how to enhance the relationships between learner and teacher, how to provide for the exceptional learner, how to evaluate learning, and how to provide for the professional development of persons within the school.

30. Egan, G. (1988). *Change-agent Skills B: Managing innovation and change*. San Diego: University Associates.

Presents a straightforward model for bringing about change in any organization. The simplicity of the change model renders it useful as the various model components or the model as a whole are considered. The formal model is based on three scenarios: current, preferred, and strategy for accomplishing change. Specific and concrete examples of change efforts are presented with each component of the model to illustrate how to implement that component within an organization.

31. English, F.W., & Hills, J.C. (1990). *Restructuring: The principal and curriculum change*. Reston, VA: The National Association of Secondary School Principals.

Presents an overview of the role of the principal as curriculum leader. Based on the restructured model of schools. Comparisons are drawn among the traditional school, the effective school, and the restructured school as a means of illustrating the developmental changes that occur as a school moves towards the restructured model. Specific issues relative to implementing change in schools illustrate how restructuring as a change process can be applied to sub-issues such as testing, dropouts, and curriculum clutter.

32. Gilchrest, R. (1989). *Effective schools: Three case studies of excellence*. Bloomington, IN: National Educational Service.

Presents findings from three case studies of schools of excellence that illustrate the profound changes that can happen when faculty are committed to excellence and helping students learn. Seven common characteristics of good schools are also discussed: positive climate, clear mission, high level of participant involvement, communication among all participants, contribution to the community, models excellence, and assessment strategies.

33. Hoyle, J.R., English, F.W., & Steffy, B.E. (1986, 1990). *Skills for successful school leaders*. Arlington, VA: American Association of School Administrators.

Offers guidelines to aid administrator preparation programs in reviewing the skills and competencies being taught in these programs. Skills in eight areas are presented with specific examples of indicators of each. The skill areas include the following: (1) developing positive school climate, (2) building support for the school, (3) curriculum development, (4) instructional management, (5) staff evaluation, (6) staff development, (7) allocation of resources, and (8) evaluation.

34. Little, J.W. (1982). Norms of collegiality and experimentation: Workplace conditions of school success. *American Educational Research Journal, 19* (3), 325–340.

Describes the research and findings relative to the characteristics of teachers' work and work conditions within the school. The findings reported clearly indicate the isolation of teachers and the lack of opportunity for collaboration and the building of collegial relationships. This seminal research suggests that experimentation and innovative activities on the part of teachers is impossible within the traditional structure of schools.

35. McCarthy, M.M., Kuh, G., Newell, L., & Iacona, C. (1988). *Under scrutiny: The educational administration professorate.* Tempe, AZ: University Council for Educational Administration.

Reports the results of a comprehensive study of educational administration faculty conducted during 1986. Attitudes and behaviors of the 1986 cohort are compared with those involved in a similar study 12 years previous. In addition, those behaviors and attitudes of the 1986 cohort are compared with those of professors in other academic fields. Interesting areas addressed in the study include activities of the educational administration professorate, characteristics and beliefs of new professors, personal and professional characteristics of all professors, and indices of change in the professorate.

36. Murphy, J. & Evertson, C. (1990). *Restructuring schools: Capturing the phenomena.* Nashville, TN: National Center for Educational Leadership, Peabody College of Education, Vanderbilt University.

Presents a paradigm for restructuring schools while highlighting such variables as teacher empowerment, shared governance, core technology, teacher work redesign, and student empowerment. The paradigm allows the change agent to see the relationships among components of a restructured school.

37. National Association of Elementary School Principals. (1990). *Principals for 21st century schools.* Alexandria, VA: National Association of Elementary School Principals.

Presents a definitive statement about the preparation of elementary and middle school principals for the next century. Based on a set of assumptions about how schools should be organized to empower participants and involve students in relevant instruction to meet their needs as workers in the twenty-first century, eleven building blocks for school leadership are presented.

38. National Association of Secondary School Principals. (1982). *The effective principal.* Reston, VA: National Association of Secondary School Principals.

In the essays of this volume, current knowledge about principals is assimilated, and practical ways to implement these ideas for increased effectiveness of school principals are suggested. The papers are part of an extensive set of literature reviews conducted for the National Institute of Education as part of its comprehensive program of work on the principalship. Topics presented include managerial leadership, research on the principalship, principals in action, and views from within the principalship.

39. National Commission on Excellence in Educational Administration. (1987). *Leaders for America's schools.* The report of the Commission on Excellence in Educational Administration. Tempe, AZ: Arizona State University and the University Council for Educational Administration.

Focuses on the improvement of educational leadership through specific recommendations. These recommendations are as follows: (1) educational leadership should be redefined; (2) a National Policy Board on Educational Administration should be established; (3) preparation programs should be modeled around those in other professional schools; (4) at least 300 university programs in educational administration should be eliminated; (5) programs for the recruitment of minorities and women should be introduced by the universities; (6) public schools should collaborate in the preparation of school leaders; (7) professional development should be an integral part of the careers of professors and practitioners; and (8) licensure programs should be reformed.

40. Rossman, G.B., Corbett, H.D., & Firestone, W.A. (1988). *Change and effectiveness in schools: A cultural perspective.* Albany, NY: State University of New York Press.

Offers a rich discussion of culture and change, recognizing that the core values and beliefs of a school greatly affect change efforts. The authors' dichotomous labeling of school norms as sacred and profane is useful to change agents in that they bring attention to sacred norms as being essentially immutable while profane norms are more susceptible to change. Case studies illustrate substantive issues in change efforts in schools.

41. Rossow, L.F. (1990). *The principalship: Dimensions in instructional leadership.* Englewood Cliffs, NJ: Prentice Hall.

Attempts to convert theory into practice by describing how principals might better function as instructional leaders in schools. Using effective schools research as a base, the author presents substantive discussions about principal instruction leadership in decision making, the curriculum, relationships with students, legal issues, effective teaching, special populations, and the school and community relations. The final chapter deals with the principal as a change agent.

42. Shea, C.M., Kahane, E., & Sola, P. (1989). *The new servants of power: A critique of the 1980s school reform movement.* Westport, CT: Greenwood Press.

Presents arguments around diverse issues in the reform movement. However, claims of equity and excellence issues were left undone. This edited book addresses the realities being mediated and rationalized by the reform reports and their impact on schools.

43. Sheive, L.T. & Schoenheit, M.B. (1987). *Leadership: Examining the elusive.* Alexandria, VA: Association for Supervision and Curriculum Development.

This yearbook highlights aspects of cultural leadership relevant to current school issues. Chapter themes include school culture, leader as change agent, women as administrators, vision, the conscience of leadership, and a theoretical base for cultural leadership.

44. Short, P.M., Greer, J.T., & Michael, R. (1991). Restructuring schools through empowerment: Facilitating the process. *Journal of School Leadership, 1* (2), 127–139.

Presents findings of a three-year national project to create empowered schools. The focus of the paper is on critical variables in the change effort. These variables may be important in two ways: (1) understanding those issues that affect efforts to substantially change the roles and responsibilities of teachers and principals toward shared governance and (2) understanding variables that change facilitators must address in efforts to assist school restructure.

45. Smith, S.C., Mazzarella, J.A., & Peile, P.K. (1985). *School leadership: Handbook for survival.* Eugene, OR: Clearinghouse on Educational Management, University of Oregon.

This edited volume, published by ERIC, addresses relevant issues centering on principal leadership in a restructured school. Chapters address issues such as site-based management, women and minority issues, team management, participative decision making, school climate, communication, stress management, managing conflict, and problem solving. Many concrete examples and ideas are presented around each topic.

46. Thomson, S.A. (1990). *Principals for our changing schools: Preparation and certification.* Report of the National Commission for the Principalship. Fairfax, VA: National Commission for the Principalship.

The National Association of Secondary School Principals and the National Association of Elementary School Principals have created the National Commission for the Principal and published recommendations for performance domains for school principals. The performance domains fall into four categories: (1) functional domains, (2) programmatic domains, (3) interpersonal domains, and (4) contextual domains. A taxonomy of standards for the school principalship is contained in the appendix.

47. Twale, D.J. & Short, P.M. (1989). Shaping school leaders for the future: Innovation in preparation. *Planning and Changing, 20* (2), 149–157.

Describes an innovative doctoral program for educational leaders that addresses some of the concerns of the National Policy Board on Educational Administration relative to collaboration with the field, socialization of students into the profession, and the development of critical problem-solving skills of school leaders. The year-long set of experiences implemented at Auburn University in the Danforth Seminar addresses these concerns. The article highlights program objectives and illustrates how various student activities within each objective relate to the development of the reflective practitioner.

48. Twombly, S. & Ebmeier, H. (1989). Educational administration programs: The cash cow of the university? In *Improving the preparation of school administrators: Notes on reform, No. 4.* Charlottesville, VA: The National Policy Board for Educational Administration.

This occasional paper discusses how resource allocation processes at universities and in schools of education trap educational administration programs in a circle of disadvantage regarding program quality and relevance. The authors contend that one of the major obstacles to the reform of administrative preparation programs is that these programs often are treated as the cash cows of universities, i.e., as low cost, resource generation units. They argue that universities must address this issue as a barrier to program reform.

CHAPTER 3

Skills Needed by Current
And Future Principals

GLOBAL SOCIETY AND THE SCHOOLS

Educational reform in the past two decades has presented new challenges for the educational leader, especially the school principal. In addition, a substantial increase of ethnic diversity in the public schools has resulted in more emphasis being placed upon developing educational administrators who understand people of other cultures, people from other countries who now reside in the United States.

The United States has been referred to as the melting pot of the world, where many cultures and ethnic groups have assimilated to form a nation. Flux in world politics, the growth of democracy in former communist countries, and the transition of the United States from creditor to debtor nation indicate a need to examine current programs for developing educational leaders.

Change and *restructuring* are two concepts which will likely affect the future of education and educational leaders in the United States. The perceptions of individuals concerning restructuring, values, diversity, future, culture/multi-culture, and the findings related to these concepts are important. At the fifth anniversary celebration of the International Education Consortium in November, 1989, in St. Louis, Ernest Boyer stated "We need to study non-Western cultures to understand our future." The future of the world belongs to all cultures and societies as illustrated by the major transformations occurring around the world—socially, economically, politically, ecologically, and culturally.

As restructuring of educational institutions occur in the United States, members of the educational administration professorate must

43

attach renewed emphasis to the development of educational leaders who understand global perspectives. Restructuring is not a rapid process and is hindered by what people do not know (Brandt, 1990; Goodlad, 1984; & Sizer, 1984). School leaders must understand and address rapid change in schools and in society. Understanding change helps create a vision to develop our nation's most precious resource—the children.

A transformation must take place in the way students, parents, and teachers perceive school restructuring in a changing world order. The principal is key to restructuring schools which will enable individuals to learn and face the complex issues of today's world. Carroll (1990) indicates that few educators are willing to face the numerous dilemmas confronting today's schools. Finn (1990) concurs that old conceptions are hard to change and that "old paradigms do not retire gracefully, and the avatars of new ones are often scorned and savaged" (p. 589).

As the role of the family changes, "changing parental values leave greater roles for educators" (Elkind, 1990, p. 8). Elkind emphasizes that school administrators must take on a greater role in the responsibility of childrearing and nurturing. School leaders must address all aspects of a child's education, including values, global perspectives, and cultural differences, as well as physical and mental performance.

Educational leaders need to be concerned with a changing society and student diversity, according to Brandt (1989). "Today's classrooms house growing numbers of poor, minority, and handicapped students," according to Hodgkinson (1988, p. 10). Changing school populations, including students from other countries and societies, require that educational processes be restructured to provide opportunities for all students. Black, Hispanic and Asian populations in the public schools symbolize a need to address a global society in American schools. Educational leaders must understand the cultural and value differences of these populations, according to Esther Taira (1989). With new Hispanic and Asian students entering the educational system every day, all will feel the effects of cultural diversity.

WORLD CHANGES

The future centers on education, new technology, and adapting to life in a global society. Cetron (1989) states that education is the key to the future for societies of all countries. Educational processes as well as the development and training of educational leaders must emphasize the changing world. Many occupations will cease to exist as new jobs are developed in a new technological society. Retooling or retraining will become a major component of schools the 1990s. Naisbitt and Aburdene

(1990) state that society must address a new world view, "this is an increasingly interconnected world . . ." (p. 15). They contend that new technology and an expanding concept of humanity become a part of global education. Economics and world politics will also become major areas of concern for educators and students in a new global economy and a peace oriented world.

As the world changes, educators in the United States need to have a better understanding of educational challenges throughout the world. Trout (1989) remarks that global education and an understanding of "glasnost" will be a challenge to educators. Reforms in the Soviet Union under Gorbachev's "perestroika" make it imperative that educational leaders understand reform concepts and how these may relate to educational processes. A changing ideology from "cold war" to coexistence offers an urgent task for educators according to Chomsky (1989). The concept of the world as a society of learners must be addressed in preparing future educational administrators.

MULTICULTURALISM

Most cultures and societies have educational processes. The educational systems may not have similar organizations or curricula, but all have a way to transmit values, beliefs, and essential knowledge to the young in the society. Since education is a common experience around the globe, it may be the most reliable vehicle for developing a common understanding and relationship among all cultures. With more international investing and interchange of business across national boundaries, new constituencies of foreign students and parents will dramatically impact educational institutions, through different needs and expectations. School principals and teachers must be prepared to work with these families in developing programs to meet the new global aspect of education.

Hunter (1990) sees the challenge for this generation of teachers and school administrators as one of generating new visions, new horizons, new definitions of the future. He goes on to propose that educators unite in recognition that education and schooling must be integrated into a world-wide system addressing not only social, economic, scientific, and religious issues, but a sensitivity to the individual cultural, social, and developmental needs of all nations.

In November 1989, Ernest L. Boyer addressed the concept of connectedness at the International Education Consortium's fifth anniversary celebration. He elaborated on the need to help students understand the economic, political, and ecological connectedness of our existence in the world. All peoples share the universal experience of birth, growth, and death. Every society uses symbols to communicate through language, has the capability to place selves in time and space, contains members of groups and institutions, and has a love of the aesthetic. In addition, producing and consuming is central to humanity. Finally, all people live by values and beliefs. Dr. Boyer proposed a planned teacher-preparation program with a core curriculum focused on human commonalities. In addition, he proposed a top-level research and development project to shape the core curriculum to give students a more coherent view of knowledge and a more integrated, more authentic view of life.

John Goodlad (1990) proposed that studying the education of teachers is essential research. He postulates that research and the preparation of teachers and educational leaders are keys to the development of good schools. Consequently, good schools must address globalistic concepts which permit coexistence in a new world. The methodology used to prepare educational leaders is obsolete.

SKILLS FOR PRINCIPALS

The educational administrator for the next century must be an individual with a global perspective, and an appreciation of all cultures, as well as be an effective leader. Preparation programs for educational administrators must provide training and development in these areas. The educational leader of this changing era must be prepared to meet the challenges of the future. New paradigms, new skills, and new competencies are required for new leaders as identified by the National Commission for the Principalship (1990). McCauley (1990) indicated that competencies demanded by educational reform must be included in principal preparation programs. With knowledge the key element for the future, Toffler (1990) states that school principals are expected to be involved in developing and implementing teacher empowerment within the school infrastructure.

Hoyle (1991) indicated that principals need both professional and personal development in order to maximize for school operations. As school principals contemplate a changing role and anticipate organizational decline (Senge, 1990), new skills are required to be effective.

The National Commission for the Principalship (1990), with a jury of fifty experts on the principalship, identified four major areas and twenty-one performance domains needed by principals of the next decade.

The four major areas are functional, programmatic, interpersonal, and contextual.

The functional domains (Thomson, 1990, 21-22) address the processes and techniques for achieving the mission and goals of the school. Educational leadership is the primary functional domain but also includes data collection, problem analysis, judgment, organizational planning, implementation, and empowerment/delegation. The skills of this domain are also reflected in information processing and decision making, setting direction, and organizing and implementing concepts to achieve goals (McCauley, 1990).

The programmatic domain focuses on the scope and framework of the educational program. The instructional program and curriculum design should reflect the educational leader's use of technology and support services for developing activities and a usable resource base. The school principal is expected to be effective in measurement and evaluation which support student achievement. Effective measurement tools and appropriate evaluation can assess principal expectations of students and faculty. Quality staff development and efficient resource allocation are necessary skills for principals (Thomson, 1990). McCauley (1990) also identifies monitoring and staff development as competencies for effective principals. Assessment is necessary to determine the school's progress toward mission and goal accomplishment, which ultimately measures a principal's leadership.

The interpersonal domain is used to illustrate the significance of human relationships, motivation, communication—both oral and written—and sensitivity to addressing both personal and professional goals (Thomson, 1990). Motivation and effective interpersonal relationships are necessary components of productive communication. Effective communication is vital to the health and harmony of the school. The school and the community must also be in contact through collaboration and mutual goals (McCauley, 1990).

The world of ideas and the forces—external and internal—on the school are reflected in the contextual domain. The philosophical and cultural values, the legal and regulatory concepts, the influences of policy, procedure and politics, and the relationships of school and community are all addressed in this domain (Thomson, 1990). Principal skills in the contextual domain involve the traditional and emerging perspectives regarding the changing role of the principal and the school.

The principal must have the competencies addressed by past research, but must also have the flexibility and adaptability to deal with future needs. The basic strategies or approaches for principal effectiveness are "motivating and reinforcing staff, building teams, creating networks, and handling pressure and stress" (McCauley, 1990, p. 13).

The following chapters examine each domain area as identified by the National Commission for the Principalship and research concerning principal skills and competencies.

NOTES

Boyer, E. (November, 1989). Fifth Anniversary Celebration. Keynote address at the International Education Consortium in St. Louis, MO.

Brandt, R. (1989). Responding differently to student differences. *Educational Leadership, 46* (6), 2.

Brandt, R. (1990). Restructuring: Where is it? *Educational Leadership, 47* (7), 3.

Carroll, J. (1990). The Copernican plan: Restructuring the American high school. *Phi Delta Kappan, 71* (5), 358-365.

Cetron, M. (1989). Class of 2000. *The School Administrator, 46* (2), 8-11.

Chomsky, N. (1989). Images of the cold war. *Educational Leadership. 46* (4), 75–78.

Elkind, D. (1990). Get ready for the post-modern family. *The School Administrator, 47* (6), 8–15.

Finn, C. (1990). The biggest reform of all. *Phi Delta Kappan, 71* (8), 584–592.

Goodlad, J. (1984). *A place called school.* New York: McGraw-Hill.

Goodlad, J. (1990). Studying the education of educators: From conception to findings. *Phi Delta Kappan, 71* (9), 698–701.

Hodgkinson, H. (1988). We must offer equal access to knowledge. *Educational Leadership, 45* (6), 10–14.

Hoyle, J.R. (1991). The principal and the pear tree. *Journal of School Leadership, 1* (2), 106–118.

Hunter, E. (1990). A vision of the future: Cooperation and courage. *NASSP Bulletin, 74* (522), 6.

McCauley, C.D. (1990). *Effective school principals: competencies for meeting the demands of educational reform.* Greensboro, NC: Center for Creative Leadership.

Naisbitt, J., & Aburdene, P. (1990). *MEGATRENDS 2000: Ten new directions for the 1990s.* New York: William Morrow and Company.

Sizer, T. (1984). *Horace's compromise: The dilemma of the American school.* Boston: Houghton Mifflin Company.

Thomson, S.A. (1990). *Principals for our changing schools: Preparation and certification.* Fairfax, VA: National Commission for the Principalship.

Taira, E. (1989). Easing Hispanics and Asians into mainstream America. *The School Administrator, 46* (1), 8–11.

Toffler, A. (1990). *Powershift: Knowledge, wealth, and violence at the edge of the 21st century.* New York: Bantam Books.

Trout, B. (1989). The educational challenge of Gorbachev's *perestroika*: What do we know? What can we teach? *Educational Leadership, 46* (4), 72–74.

Witters-Churchill, L., & Erlandson, D.A. (1990). *The principalship in the 1990's and beyond: Current research on performance-based preparation and professional development.* Tempe, AZ: The University Council for Educational Administration.

BIBLIOGRAPHY

49. Ashbaugh, C.R., & Kasten, K.L. (1991). *Educational leadership: Case studies for reflective practice.* New York: Longman.

Discusses the use of case studies in preparation programs for educational leaders. Case studies are provided for developing skills in managing people, program design and delivery, managing resources, managing external politics, and managing culture. The changing role of principals as educational leaders require effective performance skills in these domains. Case studies require skill in problem analysis and decision-making.

50. Blanton, C. (1991). A principal's vision of excellence: Achieving quality through empowerment. *Praxis,* 3 (2), 1–2, 9.

This article addresses the changing role of the principal in achieving excellence through empowerment. Identifying the research of Glasser and Deming, the author presents a set of beliefs on accomplishing goals and mission through the involvement of individuals in the work force. The author gives emphasis to empowerment and a new educational leadership for generating quality in the schools.

51. Hansen, K.H. (1988). *Decentralizing education decision making: A policy framework.* A report prepared for the Chief State School Officer of the Northwest and Pacific. Portland, OR: Northwest Center for State Education Policy Studies, Northwest Regional Educational Laboratory.

Presents findings regarding the importance of concentrating on the individual school building as the center of the change process. Policies and concepts for implementation of decision making at the school level are identified and the role of educational leaders is discussed. Policy options and how these relate to the total school program are discussed.

52. Hersey, P., & Blanchard, K.H. (1969). Life cycle theory of leadership. *Training Development Journal, 23* (5), 26–34.

The authors hypothesize that the maturity level of followers has an effect on leadership.

Hoyle, J.R. Cited above as item 13.

53. Jacobson, S.L., & Conway, J.A. (1990). *Educational leadership in an age of reform.* New York: Longman.

This edited monograph, in three parts, discusses the concepts of educational reform, the undercurrents of reform, and the preparation of school administrators to address educational reform. The future of educational leaders, especially principals, is addressed regarding the combination of instructional leadership and managerial leadership. In the last section, the direction of educational leadership is questioned as educational leaders must face the impact of new technology in schools, the reordering of educational priorities, and the rethinking of administrator preparation.

54. Mayer, J.J. (1990). *If you haven't got the **time** to do it **right**, when will you find the **time** to do it **over**?* New York: Simon and Schuster.

Time management is a key for any leader whether in business or education. The principal is provided insight into effective time management concepts and the elimination of roadblocks. Time saving strategies allow professional people to create order out of disorder.

55. McCauley, C.D. (1990). *Effective school principals: Competencies for meeting the demands of educational reform.* Greensboro, NC: Center for Creative Leadership.

The monograph is based on extensive review of research on principal effectiveness. The research on principals' skills are compared to the skills of business managers. The author identifies new challenges for principals and the need for preparation programs to address new competencies.

56. Naisbitt, J., & Aburdene, P. (1990). *Megatrends 2000: Ten new directions for the 1990's.* New York: William Morrow and Company, Inc.

Based on *Megatrends*, this new edition predicts new forces which will be transforming the world and generating a global society. The new information age is identified as a key to the patterns of confusion which must be addressed by society to achieve a meaningful future. The solution may be the contribution of each individual in establishing a purposeful course for the future.

57. Orlosky, D.E. (1988). *Society, schools, and teacher preparation.* A report of the Commission on the Future Education of Teachers for the Association of Teacher Educators. Washington, D.C.: Association of Teacher Educators and Clearinghouse on Teacher Education.

Reports the impact of reforms on education and the preparation of educators. As America enters the third millennium there will be a changing supply and demand for educators. Technology and education play a key role in the future of educators, especially the governance issues of teacher involvement in decision-making. Dynamic changes through educational reform are likely to change teacher roles in providing educational opportunities and promoting student achievement.

58.   Peters, T. (1987). *Thriving on chaos.* New York: Alfred A. Knopf.
    The contemporary and future principal will need to be able to address change, especially the chaos caused by changing factors which affect education. Roberts provides an insight into the skills managers at every level need to survive in the chaotic environments of the present and future. The prescriptions for survival in business and economic environments may be transferred to the education sphere.

59.   Prasch, J. (1990). *How to organize for school-based management.* Alexandria, VA: Association for Supervision and Curriculum Development.
    Addresses the rationale for school-based management in education. New leadership roles are defined for the principal and other educational leaders in implementing school-based management. Matrices and models are presented for implementing school-based management. Reform and societal changes are driving technology and economic globalization.

60.   Roberts, W. (1987). *Leadership secrets of Attila the Hun.* New York: Warner Books.
    Roberts offers key principles of leadership and implementing change through the "leadership secrets" of Attila the Hun. The wisdom of successful leadership through common sense guidelines provides the standards for involvement of leaders and followers in the decision making processes.

61.   Saphier, J., Bigda-Peyton, T., & Pierson, G. (1989). *How to make decisions that stay made.* Alexandria, VA: Association for Supervision and Curriculum Development.
    Reports the importance of decision making in education and presents a model for effective decision making. Factors that impede the decision-making process are presented as well as principles for overcoming such obstacles.

62.   Senge, P.M. (1990). *The fifth discipline: The art and practice of the learning organization.* New York: Doubleday Currency.
    Identifies the concepts of leadership and the skills management should have to recognize organizational disability. Teamwork coupled

with the five disciplines provides essential direction for educational leaders.

63. Short, P.M., & Spencer, W.A. (1990). Principal instructional leadership. *Journal of Research and Development in Education, 23* (2), 117–124.

This journal article describes the research and findings relative to principal leadership in effective schools. The findings indicate the perceptions of teachers and students on the leadership role of the principal that are conducive to an effective teaching/learning environment. The "environmental variables discussed include teacher support, affiliation, involvement, task orientation, order and organization, rule clarity, and teacher control."

64. Smith, W.F., & Andrews, R.L. (1989). *Instructional leadership: How principals make a difference.* Alexandria, VA: Association for the Supervision and Curriculum Development.

Presents the role of the principal as an instructional leader. Specifically identifies the role performances expected of the principal as an instructional leader, the use of the clinical supervision model, and principal evaluation. Concepts and skills required of future principals to enhance the effectiveness of educational leaders are presented.

65. Thomson, S.A. (1990). *Principals for our changing schools: Preparation and certification.* Fairfax, VA: National Commission for the Principalship.

This report focuses on the improvement of principal preparation programs for changing schools. The report identifies twenty-one [21] performance domains of the principalship. The steps for strengthening principals and the relationship of licensure and certification are discussed. The commission recognized four categories of performance domains: functional, programmatic, interpersonal, and contextual.

66. Toffler, A. (1990). *Powershift: Knowledge, wealth, and violence at the edge of the 21st century.* New York: Bantam Books.

Knowledge, wealth, and violence [force] are key components in the future of power. The book presents the meaning of power, elements of the current powershift, and outlines future struggles for power on a global front. The author encourages the use of knowledge as a base for power in the future. Educational leaders, especially principals, may be the key for implementing the powershift in education.

67. Tye, K.A. (1990). *Global education: From thought to action.* The 1991 Yearbook of the Association for Supervision and Curriculum Development. Alexandria, VA: ASCD.

An overview of the concepts related to leadership roles in implementing global education. The conflicts, the development, and the impact of global education on educational leadership roles are explored. The consequences of curriculum considerations for a global society indicate a key role for the principal and other educational leaders.

68. Witters-Churchill, L., & Erlandson, D.A. (1990). *The principalship in the 1990's and beyond: Current research on performance-based preparation and professional development.* Tempe, AZ: The University Council for Educational Administration.

Addresses the research from several states on performance-based preparation of principals and the concepts for assessing these skills. Preparation programs and skills training in these programs provide a skill base for future principals. A comparison of four case studies and an evaluation of principal performance leave an unanswered dilemma for future preparation programs.

SECTION TWO
FUNCTIONAL SKILLS

CHAPTER 4
Leadership

INTRODUCTION

Functional leadership is distinct from the broad, overarching dimensions of leadership in schools in that it focuses on the daily facilitation of groups and individuals toward task accomplishment. Broad leadership is the influencing of "school cultures by building a vision, stimulating innovation, and encouraging performance" (National Commission on the Principalship, 1990, p. 21). However, functional leadership requires daily attention to maintaining group function, setting priorities, insuring that tasks are completed, and building staff ideas into school tasks.

Leadership in Decision Groups

To facilitate the achievement of group tasks within the school organization, principals must be knowledgeable about group dynamics. Yukl (1990) suggests two types of positive group behavior: task-oriented and group maintenance-oriented behavior. Task-oriented behaviors include structuring, stimulating communication, clarifying communication, summarizing, and consensus testing (Yukl, 1990). Examples of group-maintenance behaviors are gatekeeping, harmonizing, supporting, standard setting, and process analyzing (Yukl, 1990).

Understanding these behaviors and their subsequent role in group process allows principals to facilitate group activities and maximize group effectiveness. The role of principal as director, driver, and controller becomes one of facilitator in group-centered activities within the school. Research in business and industry has shown that self-managing teams increase worker sense of contribution, empowerment, and subsequent satisfaction with being in the organization (Hackman, 1986).

Hackman (1986) characterized self-managing work groups as collections of people who take personal responsibility for the outcomes of their work, monitor their own performance and seek ways to improve it, seek needed resources from the organization, and take the initiative to help others improve (Hackman, 1986). Tom Peters (1987, p. 181) states, "there is no limit to what the average person can accomplish if thoroughly involved . . . this can most effectively be tapped when people are gathered in human-scale groupings—that is, teams, or more precisely, self-managing teams."

Lawler (1986) noted that two kinds of training are essential for members of self-managing work groups, training in the task and training in interpersonal skills. Researchers also have been interested in the functions of leaders in organizations with self-managing teams. Most writers on the subject have concluded that leadership is at least as important in organizations with self-managing work groups as it is in traditionally structured organizations (Hackman, 1986; Lawler, 1986; Manz & Sims, 1987). Leadership is, however, different. Manz and Sims (1984) describe the leader in an organization with self-managing work groups as an "unleader," "one who leads others to lead themselves" (p. 411). Hackman (1986) noted that "leadership is both more important and a more demanding undertaking in self-managing units than in traditional organizations" (p. 119). These findings relate to facilitative principal leadership in an empowered school.

Group-centered leadership requires that principals do more listening to and observing of the needs, feelings, and ideas of all participants in the school (Yukl, 1990). Principals must also become consultants, model leadership for others, and establish a climate that encourages risk taking and experimentation. Ultimately, the group should have the authority to make the final decision if teachers are to embrace risk taking and experimentation.

Leadership in Planning for Change

One of the most critical leadership tasks for the principal is to involve the school and community in planning for change. McCoy & Alfred (1985) have developed a model of involvement called the Purpose Identification Model.

The steps in the model include the following: (1) selection of a committee for quality assurance to guide the identification of activities and suggest recommendations; (2) survey of all population groups relative to feelings and beliefs about what needs to be done; (3) analyze current activity and its rationale; (4) analyze proposed suggestions using experts; (5) assimilate all input and make changes; and (6) evaluate periodically (McCoy & Alfred, 1985).

Rossow (1990) suggests that principals should be aware that their efforts at leading groups through change will involve seven steps: awareness, initiation, implementation, routinization, refinement, renewal, and evaluation.

NOTES

Hackman, J.R. (1986). The psychology of self-management in organizations. In M.S. Pollack & O. Perloff (Eds.), *Psychology and Work: Productivity, Change, and Employment*. Washington, DC: American Psychological Association.

Hackman, J.R., & Oldham, G.R. (1980). *Work redesign*. Reading, MA: Addison-Wesley.

Lawler, E.E., III. (1986). *High involvement management: Participative strategies for improving organizational performance*. San Francisco, CA: Jossey-Bass.

Manz, C.C., & Sims, H.P., Jr. (1987). Leading workers to lead themselves: The external leadership of self-managing work teams. *Administrative Science Quarterly, 32* (1), 106–128.

Manz, C.C., & Sims, H.P., Jr. (1984). Searching for the "unleader": Organizational member views on leading self-managing groups. *Human Relations, 37* (1), 409–424.

McCoy, J.W., & Alfred, W.E. (1985). Balance purposes, processes to achieve effective change. *NASSP Bulletin, 69* (473), 4.

Peters, T. (1987). *Thriving on chaos: Handbook for a management revolution*. New York: Alfred Knopf.

Rossow, L.F. (1990). *The principalship: Dimension in instructional leadership*. Englewood Cliffs, NJ: Prentice-Hall.

Thomson, S.A. (1990). *Principals for our changing schools: Preparation and certification*. Report of the National Commission for the Principalship. Fairfax, VA: National Commission for the Principalship.

Yukl, G.A. (1990). *Leadership in organizations*. Englewood Cliffs, NJ: Prentice-Hall.

BIBLIOGRAPHY

69. Broadwell, M.M. (1979). Moving up to supervision. *Training and Development Journal, 33* (2), 12–18.
This article contains information for prospective supervisors on how to develop skills in the areas of delegating, communicating, appraising, and training. Specifically, delegation is presented from the perspective of rationale, authority, responsibility, and accountability.

70. Cunard, R. F. (1990). Sharing instructional leadership—A view of strengthening the principals' position. *NASSP Bulletin, 74* (525), 30–34.
The role of the principal as an instructional leader is discussed. Suggestions are provided to assist the principal in sharing instructional leadership with teachers. Examples include assigning staff development roles of teachers, creating an instructional council, an instructional dean's position, and the utilization of peer coaching.

71. Hackman, J.R. (1986). The psychology of self-management in organizations. In M.S. Pollack & O. Perloff (Eds.), *Psychology and Work: Productivity Change and Employment,* (pp. 85-136). Washington, DC: American Psychological Association.
This piece, in a collection of work dealing with the psychology of work and productivity, details how self-managing teams operate in organizations and the psychological underpinnings that facilitate their development.

72. Hanny, R.J. (1987). Use but don't abuse, the principles of instructional effectiveness. *Clearing House, 60* (5), 209–211.
A strong case is made for the principal to function effectively as an instructional leader. Principals should be well versed in curriculum development, teacher effectiveness, clinical supervision, staff development, and teacher evaluation.

73. Kirkwood, A.A. (1990). *The role of the principal as a manager of conflict resolution.* (ERIC Document Reproduction Service No. ED 321 373)
Contrasts the traditional approach to minimizing conflict with a view of conflict as inevitable, functional, and manageable. Guidelines are provided for dealing with conflict involving students, teachers, parents, and the community.

74. Lawler, E.E., III. (1986). *High involvement management: Participative strategies for improving organizational performance.* San Francisco, CA: Jossey-Bass.

This book presents ways to provide for participative decision making and involvement in organizations as a means to increase worker ownership and commitment.

75. Lyman, L.R. (1988). *The principal: Responsive leadership in times of change.* Paper presented at the annual meeting of United School Administrators of Kansas, Wichita, KS. (ERIC Document Reproduction Service No. ED 293 201).

The personal and professional qualities of effective leaders are discussed in this comprehensive paper which examines the role of the principal in today's ever changing schools. Lyman includes eleven attributes of administrators that promote effective school practices.

76. Lyons, J.E. (1990). Managing stress in the principalship. *NASSP Bulletin, 74* (523), 44–47.

Provides suggestions for the daily management of stress by secondary school principals. Principals are advised to delegate responsibility, redefine their supervisory role, establish a personal network, and engage in stress-reducing activities.

77. Manz, C.C., & Sims, H.P., Jr. (1987). Leading workers to lead themselves: The external leadership of self-managing work teams. *Administrative Science Quarterly, 32* (1), 106–128.

Examines the issues and behaviors of leadership in organizations that use self-managing teams and presents research findings.

78. Manz, C.C., & Sims, H.P., Jr. (1984). Searching for the "unleader": Organizational member views on leading self-managing groups. *Human Relations, 37* (1), 409–424.

Presents findings of research directed at identifying how workers in self-managing teams view effective leaders and leader behavior.

79. McCoy, J.W., & Alfred, W.E. (1985). Balance purposes, processes to achieve effective change. *NASSP Bulletin, 69* (473), 4.

Offers ideas for the school principal relative to systematically organizing change.

Peters, T. Cited above as item 59.

80. Rogus, J.F. (1990). Developing a vision statement—some considerations for principals. *NASSP Bulletin, 74* (523), 6–12.

Outlines procedures that can be utilized by principals to develop and clarify a school mission statement or a vision for the future. Included are guidelines for working with faculty and interested constituents.

81. Rogus, J.F. (1988). Instructional leadership: An informal approach. *NASSP Bulletin, 72* (510), 17-22.

Provides principals with effective leadership strategies that can be utilized on an informal day-to-day basis to supplement formal program activities. A program is outlined based on commitments that must be made by the principal.

Rossow, L.F. Cited above as item 41.

82. Starratt, R.J. (1988). Administrative leadership in policy review and evaluation. *Educational Evaluation and Policy Analysis, 10* (2), 141–150.

Provides arguments for expanding the traditional roles of school administrators, including reviewing and evaluating policy.

83. Ubben, G.C., & Hughes, L.W. (1987). *The principal: Creative leadership for effective schools.* Newton, MA: Allyn & Bacon.

The relationship between creative administrative leadership and effective schooling is supported in the research literature. The personal skills and attributes of effective leaders shape the organizational environment in which teaching and learning are facilitated. The chapters in this book are organized into four parts which address the following issues: (1) the organizational and societal settings in schools which promote effective schooling; (2) the curriculum and students; (3) human resource management skills; and (4) the tools and techniques for effective school management.

84. Yukl, G.A. (1990). *Leadership in organizations.* Englewood Cliffs, NJ: Prentice-Hall.

A comprehensive overview of leadership theories including definitive studies in leadership.

CHAPTER 5

Information Collection

INTRODUCTION

Processing enough key data is important to any decision made in the operation of the school. Information sources are abundant if the principal understands where and how to collect data essential in long and short-term decisions. In addition, data gathering is a critical variable in successful and creative solutions to school problems.

Schmuck and Runkel (1988) have suggested that data gathering should occur in problem solving, communication, conflict management, and decision making. In addition, data gathering should help determine program effectiveness and goal attainment in the school organization. Finally, data gathering is critical in determining contextual influences on the school.

Data Gathering in Decision Making

While most principals are aware that data must be gathered in order to make decisions, reasons for this critical activity may remain unclear. In the decision making process, data collection includes gathering reliable, objective information, from multiple sources (Rossow, 1990) which will affect the quality of the decisions. Rossow (1990) also suggests that this process will require certain skills on the part of the principal. These include listening abilities and interpersonal communication skills.

The data gathering process should include self-reflection by the principal to determine what information is currently available and what information is needed. Principals, in consultation with others, need to determine possible data sources as well as accessibility to the data (Rossow, 1990). Professional journals, current research findings, colleagues, prior experience, and other sources often provide avenues which suggest information important to any decision. Schmuck and Runkel (1988) postulate that principal observation of the organization is a critical source of data for decision making about the school.

Data gathering about how the organization makes decisions can be an important activity for the principal. Data concerning teacher involvement, role clarity, and teacher alienation in decision making are necessary for understanding the effectiveness of the process in a particular school (Schmuck & Runkel, 1988). In addition, teacher perceptions regarding influence in decision making may be helpful.

Decision Making in Communication

An often overlooked area where process data would be important is school-wide communication. Particularly in schools where participative decision making and shared governance are the norm, communication becomes complex (Short, Greer, & Michael, 1991). Research in empowered schools suggests that communication becomes multi-directional, including dialogue across decision-making teams and among all organizational participants (Short et al., 1991).

Data sources that are important in understanding organizational communication include observations of how teachers and staff interact both informally and formally. It is important to note active listening skills of participants, group process skills within the school, and the amount of conflict that occurs as a result of poor communication and lack of information. In addition, teacher and staff perceptions about communication and flow of information in the school may be gathered through questionnaires and interviews. Rating forms may be administered to school decision-making teams that gather data regarding group member participation. When conflicts occur within the team, data relative to participant perceptions concerning communication effectiveness are critical in understanding what went wrong (Schmuck & Runkel, 1988).

Data Gathering in Conflict Management

Conflict is a way of life in organizations and schools are no exception. Conflicts can occur at the school-wide level, between groups within the organization, and among individuals in the school (Schmuck & Runkel, 1988). Yukl (1990) suggests that a primary role of the leader is to encourage those in conflict to resolve conflicts in a constructive manner, or at least to manage the conflict. Conflict can create times of instability which can be used to create change and movement within the organization. Therefore, conflict management recognizes the positive role that conflict may play within the school organization.

Principals can use conflict to successfully create change if they understand the nature of the conflict and issues involved. Certain data which focus on collaborative relationships within the school, level of participant interdependence in accomplishing school tasks, and organizational climate are critical elements in helping inform the principal about the organization (Schmuck and Runkel, 1988).

Asking teachers and staff to characterize the quality of collaboration within the school and among various school units should provide critical data for use in conflict management (Schmuck & Runkel, 1988). In addition, information about the degree to which those in conflict must work together on a daily basis may inform decisions about conflict management and resolution.

Organizational climate data may indicate the degree to which teachers perceive the school as a healthy and productive environment. Such a survey may identify policies which impede a positive atmosphere as well as areas where participants believe that they are excluded or discounted. A climate survey may reveal the extent to which teachers enjoy each other on a professional and personal basis. Finally, a climate assessment can suggest areas of potential and existing conflict and dislike.

Data Gathering in Problem Solving

Data gathering in order to solve problems centers upon information both in problem framing and identification as well as problem solution. Schmuck and Runkel (1988) posit that much of the data gathering conducted by principals around communication, group effectiveness, decision making processes, and conflict management are useful in problem solving.

However, there exists additional data that may be useful in problem finding and problem solving. Principals may find it important to interview teachers and staff to ascertain perceptions about what the school is not doing, surprising information about the school heard elsewhere, ways in which the school might operate more effectively and efficiently, and ways in which the school is changing (Schmuck & Runkel, 1988). In addition, data on perceptions of school goals and activities may be helpful. Because group effectiveness may be at the heart of successful problem solving in schools, data regarding teacher perceptions about how well groups accomplish tasks and members' level of participation is critical (Schmuck & Runkel, 1988).

Data gathering is an important task for principals. Reliable and objective information will facilitate better problem solving and decision making in organizations. For schools to function effectively, information useful in managing conflict, developing communication processes, and framing problems must be gathered from multiple sources. Principal skills in accomplishing this are critical.

NOTES

Rossow, L.F. (1990). *The principalship: Dimensions in instructional leadership.* Englewood Cliffs, NJ: Prentice Hall.

Schmuck, R., & Runkel, P. (1988). *The handbook of organization development in schools.* Prospect Hills, IL: Waveland Press.

Short, P.M., Greer, J.T., & Michael, R. (1991). Restructuring schools empowerment: Facilitating the process. *Journal of School Leadership, 1* (2), 127–139.

Yukl, G.A. (1990). *Leadership in organizations.* Englewood Cliffs, NJ: Prentice Hall.

BIBLIOGRAPHY

85. Lindle, F.C. (1989). Market analysis identifies community and school education goals. *NASSP Bulletin, 73* (520), 62–66.
Provides an overview for marketing the schools and how marketing can be utilized to improve the school program and gain support. A description of the four phases of marketing is also included.

86. McColskey, W.H., et al. (1985). Predictors of principals' reliance on formal and informal sources of information. *Educational Evaluation and Policy Analysis, 7* (4), 427–436.
This article reports a study that investigated secondary school principals' use of information for decision making. Results showed that data use distinguished between greater and lesser information users.

87. McIntyre, H. (1985). Setting the tone for your school: Advice for the first-year principal. *NASSP Bulletin, 69* (480), 85–90.
The success of the first-year principal is enhanced when the administrator acquires a comprehensive understanding of the organizational dynamics of the school. McIntyre outlines a five-step approach for the first-year principal.

88. Schmuck, R. & Runkel, P. (1988). *The handbook of organization development in schools.* Prospect Hills, IL: Waveland Press.
While presenting a wide range of information on how to change schools through organizational development, this book describes issues in decision making that involve data gathering.

Short, P.M., Greer, J.T., & Michael, R. Cited above as item 44.

Starratt, R.J. Cited above as item 82.

Yukl, G. A. Cited above as item 84.

CHAPTER 6
Problem Analysis

INTRODUCTION

Problems arise in schools out of frustration resulting from discrepancies between desired situations and the current state of affairs. These frustrations may eventually involve all aspects of organizational life. In facing and solving problems, principals must analyze all aspects of the organization to provide leadership which will deal with problems and frustrations.

However, having problems in schools can also be healthy for the organization, as an opportunity to contemplate change and take action (Schmuck & Runkel, 1988). In approaching problems, principals may find it useful to view them as having three aspects: the present situation, the desired state, and the paths that might be taken to arrive at the desired state (Schmuck & Runkel, 1988). These three approaches provide the basis for problem analysis designed to bring about conflict resolution. Framing and evaluating are two techniques principals can use in problem analysis.

Problem Framing

Problem definition or framing may be the most critical step in problem analysis since the manner in which the problem is characterized affects possible alternative solutions. Rossow (1990) suggests that problem framing must not be rushed. At first glance, the information presented may be incorrect and/or biased. The principal must spend time gathering relevant, objective information.

Gorton (1980) suggests that in the early stages of problem framing that the principal determine what is known and unknown about the issues. The principal must attempt to clarify significant factors surrounding the situation. Secondly, the principal should identify data sources and determine their objectivity. Further, Gorton (1980) recommends that the principal analyze the seriousness of the problem, including the need for quick decisions in problem resolution.

Problem Evaluation

An additional technique in problem analysis is to evaluate the need for action. In some situations, one viable alternative may be to do nothing, which is making a decision (Rossow, 1990). In other instances, where a decision is needed, someone other than the principal should make the decision (Rossow, 1990).

At this stage in problem analysis, the principal may wish to engage in brainstorming. Involving others in brainstorming alternative solutions can increase the amount and quality of data available. Seeking relevant information may be one of the most important activities of the principal during problem analysis.

NOTES

Gorton, R.A. (1980). *School administration and supervision.* Dubuque, IA: William C. Brown.

Rossow, L.F. (1990). *The principalship: Dimensions in instructional leadership.* Englewood Cliffs, NJ: Prentice-Hall.

Schmuck, R., & Runkel, P. (1988). *The handbook of organization development in schools.* Prospect Hills, IL: Waveland Press.

BIBLIOGRAPHY

89. Gorton, R.A. (1980). *School administration and supervision.*
     Dubuque, IA: William C. Brown.
     This book covers traditional issues in school administration and
provides helpful discussions on problem analysis in the administrative
context.

     Kirkwood, A.A. Cited above as item 73.

90. Leithwood, K.A., & Stager, M. (1989). Expertise in principals'
     problem solving. *Educational Administration Quarterly, 25* (2),
     126–161.
     Report of a study designed to investigate cultural elements in
problem solving by school principals. The authors interviewed 22
elementary school principals and compared their responses to hypothetical
case problems. Differences were noted between experts and their typical
colleagues.

91. Leithwood, K.A., & Stager, M. (1986, April). *Differences in
     problem-solving processes used by moderately and highly effective
     principals.* Paper presented at the annual meeting of the American
     Educational Research Association, San Francisco, CA. (ERIC
     Document Reproduction Service No. ED 269 881)
     Results of a study designed to investigate problem-solving
strategies among elementary school principals are presented. There were
significant differences between the two groups in the strategies they
utilized to solve problems and in their perceptions regarding the
influences of various factors on their problem-solving.

     Lyons, J.E. Cited above as item 76.

     Rossow, L.F. Cited above as item 41.

     Schmuck, R., & Runkel, P. Cited above as item 88.

92. Taylor, B.O. (1986). *How and why successful elementary school
     principals address strategic issues.* Paper presented at the annual
     meeting of the American Educational Research Association, San
     Francisco, CA. (ERIC Document Reproduction Service No. ED
     278 124)
     Common patterns of decision-making processes are examined as a
result of a three year investigation analyzing the thinking and language

patterns of 22 "effective change" elementary school principals. These change agents share a common knowledge base which includes a capacity for change, ability to effectively interact with others, and use strategic dialogues.

CHAPTER 7
Judgment

INTRODUCTION

The ability to exercise judgment in both actions and decisions is essential for principals. Critical aspects of judgment can include exercising caution in situations where additional data are needed before making a decision. In addition, good judgment requires that principals are aware of those situations where priority must be given.

Types of Judgment

Jung's work on perception and judgment (Read, Fordham, & Adler, 1970) suggests that there are two types of judgment: thinking and feeling. Tendencies of individuals toward one or the other type may impact decision making (Read et al., 1970).

Thinking Type of Judgment

Those principals who enjoy evaluating situations by logic may be thinking types. Pertinent facts about the situation or activity, timelines towards completion of projects, and details about processes are more interesting and important to thinking types than any other outcomes (Read et al., 1970).

Feeling Type of Judgment

In contrast to the thinking type of judgment, principals who are the feeling type rely more readily upon the interpersonal aspect of their positions. They are much more concerned with the philosophical aspects of decision making and how situations affect the way people feel (Read et al, 1970). How they feel about an issue is more critical than logical facts or rational processes.

NOTES

Read, H., Fordham, M., & Adler, G. (1970). *Carl Jung: Collected works.* Princeton, NJ: Princeton University Press.

BIBLIOGRAPHY

Cunard, R.F. Cited above as item 70.

93. Garten, T., & Valentine, J. (1989). Strategies for faculty involvement in effective schools. *NASSP Bulletin, 73* (515), 1–6.
Description of three strategies that can be utilized by principals in goal setting and implementation. Specifically, suggestions are provided on how to involve faculty in the goal setting through building-level committees and administrative-improvement councils.

Kirkwood, A. A. Cited above as item 73.

Leithwood, K.A., & Stager, M. Cited above as item 90.

Leithwood, K.A., & Stager, M. Cited above as item 91.

94. Lohr, C., & McGrevin, C. (1990). Scheduling: The blueprint for educational success. *NASSP Bulletin, 74* (529), 83–89.
Emphasizes the importance of the master schedule at the building level as an instructional tool. Educational philosophy, a collegial working relationship between principal and faculty and school climate contribute to the development of a successful master schedule.

95. Lysak, B., & Lee, B. (1991). Bullies, whiners—You know the type. Here's how to handle them. *Executive Educator, 13* (4), 18-19, 27.
Difficult people exist everywhere as bullies, "yes" people, whiners, nonentities, know-it-alls, or "no" people. These six personality types are examined by the authors, including techniques for principals to use in dealing with each type.

McColskey, W.H., et al. Cited above as item 86.

96. Newberry, A.J.H. (1982). SOCIOfutures, TECHNOfutures, and BIOfutures. *Education Canada, 22* (2), 12-15.
Intelligence, group skills, scholarship, mature judgment, good health, and personal security provide the necessary survival skills for principals. Eight professional survival skills—human relations, communications, community relations, administrative technical, decision making, research, curriculum development, and change strategy skills—are also important.

97. Read, H., Fordham, M., & Adler, G. (1970). *Carl Jung: Collected works*. Princeton, NJ: Princeton University Press.

A comprehensive discussion of Jung's theories relative to judgment in human action and behavior. Some of the discussion has relevance to administrative decision making and judgment.

Rossow, L.F. Cited above as item 41.

Rogus, J.F. Cited above as item 81.

Taylor, B.O. Cited above as item 92.

CHAPTER 8
Organizational Oversight

INTRODUCTION

In order to carry out the responsibilities of the principalship, it is important that principals have skills in planning and organizing. Both short- and long-range planning provide a framework for accomplishing the goals of the organization. Planning facilitates utilization of resources to meet the goals of the school. In addition, planning requires monitoring the work of the organization toward goals and objectives.

Principals should have knowledge of the various types of planning that can be carried out within the school. They also should know how to set short and long term goals for the school. Principals' abilities in establishing action plans should be extensive.

Three Types of Planning

All planning carried out at the school building level should be tied to district goals and objectives. With this in mind, there are three types of planning processes available to the school principal.

Operational planning or short-range planning may cover a time frame of several months to a year. This type of planning should be used to deal with routine matters within the school. Lewis (1983) suggests that operational planning is the "process of identifying a need, setting short-range objectives, detailing performance standards, and describing an action plan (p. 10). Lewis (1983) presents examples of items developed in the operational planning process: professional improvement plans by teachers and for the school, individual performance plans, and monitoring charts such as Gantt and PERT charts which lead to school or group short-range plans.

A second type of planning process useful to the principal is problem-solving planning. Lewis (1983) suggests that this type of planning should last no longer than several months. It involves identifying a problem that adversely affects the routine performance of a school, choosing a strategy for alleviating the problem, outlining monitoring and assessment plans, implementing the plan for no longer than 30 days if possible.

In problem-solving planning, a critical step in the process is the analysis of the problem. Lewis (1983) suggests that this analysis be broken down into four steps: description of the problem, data gathering, determining the causes, and proposed action.

Advantages to problem-solving planning may include catching little problems early, staff involvement, development of creativity of staff in finding solutions to problems, staff ownership of problems and problem solutions, and systematic approach to dealing with problems within the school (Lewis, 1983).

Long-range planning or strategic planning may cover a time frame from three to ten years. It usually includes needs assessments, goal setting and goal consensus activities, and may involve the school community in the planning process. Lewis states that long range planning is the process of "realizing the school organization's mission, long-range goals, and strategies governing use of human and nonhuman resources needed to achieve the mission" (1983, p. 10).

Two models of long-range planning include what Lewis calls the instructional program model and the comprehensive model (1983). The instructional program model is the most widely used in schools and includes setting educational goals and objectives, a needs assessment, selecting or changing instructional programs as determined by needs assessment, and evaluation (Lewis, 1983).

The comprehensive model is more extensive and includes a critical analysis of the internal and external environment, developing planning assumptions, selecting long-range goals, identifying program strategies, and initiating operational planning and problem-solving planning where needed (Lewis, 1983). This type of planning is intensive, requires a great deal of time, and involves various groups of persons throughout the school, district, and community. However, these comprehensive plans should be open to revision throughout the two to ten years for which they are developed. Environmental scanning has become a necessary part of long-term or strategic planning in many large school districts.

Action Plans

Action planning involves the implementation of plans and decisions that have been made. Hoy and Miskel (1991) suggest that there are four parts to the action plan. The first part includes programming, the mechanics or details about how the plan is to take place. Part two includes communicating, or the dissemination of plan responsibilities and timelines so that others can carry out their assigned roles. Monitoring, part three, is the process of overseeing the implementation of the plan. This is a control process that includes a feedback loop (Hoy & Miskel, 1991). Appraising, the fourth step, involves the assessment of the effectiveness of the implemented plan or decision and may actually initiate the entire process over again (Hoy & Miskel, 1991).

Planning for Instructional Leadership

There are key issues in planning for instructional leadership as outlined in the NASSP model, *Leader 123*. Key behaviors of principals who wish to improve their instructional leadership skills through planning include identifying the instructional leadership opportunity, obtaining relevant information, identifying the criteria for determining that the problem is resolved, deciding whether a long or short term solution is needed, developing an overall strategy, identifying key personnel, establishing timelines, and setting a measurable objective (NASSP, 1990).

Principals' skills in planning are critical for the management of change within the school. Principals should be aware of the three types of planning and how each may be used in effectively carrying out the mission of the school.

NOTES

Hoy, W., & Miskel, C. (1991). *Educational administration: Theory, research, and practice.* New York: McGraw-Hill.

Lewis, J. (1983). *Long-range and short-range planning for educational administrators.* Boston: Allyn and Bacon.

National Association of Secondary School Principals. (1990). *Leader 1 2 3: Professional development program in instructional leadership for school administrators.* Training manual. Reston, VA: NASSP.

BIBLIOGRAPHY

Cunard, R.F. Cited above as item 70.

Garten, T., & Valentine, J. Cited above as item 93.

Hanny, R.J. Cited above as item 72.

98. Hord, S.M., & Huling-Austin, L. (1986). Effective curriculum intervention: Some promising new insights. *Elementary School Journal, 87* (1), 97–115.
   Facilitating change in schools is a key element in school reform. Results of a principal-teacher interaction study are discussed in terms of how programs are implemented when principals and faculty cooperatively plan new school programs.

99. Hoy, W., & Miskel, C. (1991). *Educational administration: Theory, research, and practice.* New York: McGraw-Hill.
   This important text on school administration is a comprehensive discussion of both research and theory in educational administration.

100. Hughes, L., & Ubben, G. (1984). *The elementary principal's handbook.* Boston: Allyn and Bacon.
   This outstanding book presents practical suggestions to principals on planning, including action planning. Various charts and diagrams provide useful ways to carry out the planning process in the school.

101. Lewis, J. (1983). *Long-range and short-range planning for educational administrators.* Boston: Allyn and Bacon.
   This book is a comprehensive overview of three types of planning in school organizations. These three types include action planning/problem-solving planning, long-range planning, and operational planning. Many tables, charts, and diagrams make this a very useful book to the practitioner.

Lohr, C., & McGrevin, C. Cited above as item 94.

102. Martin, R.J. (1987). Cooperative planning and goal implementation. *Reading Psychology, 8* (4) 319–325.
   Report of an elementary school project in Richardson, Texas, demonstrating the positive effects that occur through cooperative planning between teachers and the principal. The results of the project showed that the instructional program had improved.

103.   Michael, S.R. (1979). Control, contingency and delegation in decision-making. *Training and Development Journal, 33* (2), 36–42.

A risk management model is provided which stresses delegating decision-making authority and managerial control. Six specific strategies to reduce risk taking are provided.

104.   National Association of Secondary School Principals. (1990). *Leader 1 2 3: Professional development program in instructional leadership for school administrators.* Training Manual. Reston, VA: NASSP.

This outstanding development and training program in instructional leadership for principals includes specific key behaviors in planning.

105.   Rees, R. (1987). *Delegation—A fundamental management process.* (ERIC Document Reproduction Service No. ED 294 330).

Approaches are offered for the effective use of delegation procedures by school administrators. Provides a description of the steps in the delegation process, which includes task identification, assessment of skills needed, selection of subordinates, task assignments, identification of resources, monitoring, and feedback.

Rogus, J.F. Cited above as item 81.

Rossow, L.F. Cited above as item 41.

106.   Rutherford, W.L. (1984). Styles and behaviors of elementary school principals: The relationship to school improvement. *Education and Urban Society, 17* (1), 9–28.

A discussion of principal effectiveness based on principal behavior. Principals who are perceived as being the most effective are those who provide active, visible leadership and closely monitor the goals that are designed to bring about improvement in the school program.

107.   Snyder, K.J. (1988). Managing a productive school work culture. *NASSP Bulletin, 72* (510), 40–43.

The author provides a review of common cultural dimension themes on management. Included is information on symbol systems, group sharing and networking, reward and recognition systems, and empowerment.

108. Staven, L.L. (1982). Administrative behavior that will get things done. *NASSP Bulletin, 66* (455), 121–122.

Provides a description of an effective administrator. Primary characteristic is one who can function in a variety of roles (e.g. consultant, catalyst, group resource) but will take risks and expects to be misunderstood occasionally.

CHAPTER 9
Implementation

INTRODUCTION

Implementation involves putting into action those plans developed to bring about change in the school (Schmuck & Runkel, 1988). Principals engage in change efforts on a daily basis. Efforts to bring about change through innovation is perhaps one of the greatest challenges to principals. Principal skills at implementing innovation are critical. However, planned change efforts require consideration of a number of variables.

Components of Planned Change

Hanson (1991) has identified three components of planned change. Principals must first understand the technology of the innovation or new effort which requires time and energy in learning about new approaches. The second component centers around developing an understanding of the constraints within the school environment to the implementation of the innovation. Taking time to analyze the forces that might impede implementation enables principals to plan strategies to alleviate the resistance. The third component involves a strategy for change. This critical component suggests that principals must develop clear tactics for involving participants in the change effort, for eroding resistance to the innovation, for securing resources to support the innovation, and for training, preparation, and planning by the participants. In addition, it suggests that principals should establish mechanisms for checking progress of the change effort, providing mid-course corrections, and adapting to new conditions.

Focus of Change

Hanson (1991) has pointed out that change efforts can be focused on a number of school variables. These include the tasks of the organization, the organizational structure such as departments, the technology of the organization such as teaching, and the people in the school.

When considering implementing change focused on any of these variables, it is important to note that they can be interdependent (Hanson, 1991). Efforts to change the technology of teaching through the implementation of cooperative learning also requires changes in people— their attitudes and skills. However, Katz and Kahn (1966) suggest that principals must distinguish between change efforts focused on the individual level and those at the organizational level. Even more critical is the need to focus change efforts simultaneously on both levels. Implementation problems occur when principals work on individuals in the change effort and place them back into an organizational structure that does not facilitate the new skills and expectations of the individual (Katz & Kahn, 1966). Implementation problems also occur when the organizational structure of the school is modified with no corresponding change in the attitudes and behaviors of teachers.

Resistance to Change

Principals may meet resistance to implementation efforts on two levels: organizational and individual (Hanson, 1991). At the organizational level, the bureaucratic structure of schools, by their very nature, may impede implementation of change strategies. This is due to the hierarchical, standardized roles within the organization as well as values of control and top—down communication ((Hanson, 1991).

An additional organizational variable causing resistance to change is the lack of clear goals for schools. In this sense, there is little agreement about school purpose. Finally, Hanson (1991) suggests that implementation of change may be difficult in schools due to lack of measurable cost relative to benefits derived from the change.

At the individual level, variables affecting implementation of change can include vested interest in a particular program or project that may be the focus of the change effort (Hanson, 1991). Other individual characteristics may impede change, including whether individuals see themselves as upwardly mobile within the school, suggesting a propensity to conform to school goals and norms (Hanson, 1991). Also, individual risk-taking and experimentation tendencies influence a person's acceptance of change.

Change Models

Chin and Benne (1969) present three change models that have relevance to schools. The rational-empirical model suggests that groups are rational and will embrace change if presented with enough information that shows that the change is justified. Principals wishing to implement change based on this model would ply teachers with information on the innovation and tell them how much the innovation is needed.

The second change model, normative-reeducative, is based on the premise that behaviors are influenced by norms, interpersonal relationships, and attitudes (Chin & Benne, 1969). Approaches to change would aim at changing feelings and values about the innovation through involvement and group activities.

The x suggests that change occurs when the threat of sanctions are used. Rules, regulations, laws, and loss of resources are tactics useful in this change model (Chin & Benne, 1969).

Role of Interactions in Implementation

Implementation of change within schools implies the interaction between environment and innovation (Hanson, 1991). Mutual adaptation implies modification and simplification of the innovation, or the revision of expectations about the innovation (Hanson, 1991).

Another result of the interaction between environment and individual may be non-implementation. This implies that no adaptation occurs and the innovation is overcome by implementation problems (Hanson, 1991). A third pattern from this interaction may be coaptation or change in the project or innovation but no change within the individuals involved in the innovation.

Key Behaviors for Implementation

Key behaviors for implementation by the principal have been identified by the National Association of Secondary School Principals in the *Leader 123* developmental program in instructional leadership

(NASSP, 1990). These behaviors include communicating needed information to people, following a plan, collecting data to monitor project status, anticipating unfavorable outcomes, diffusing conflict, and celebrating successes (NASSP, 1990).

Principal skills in implementation are critical for change to occur in schools. Principal knowledge about planned change can enhance the chances that implementation strategies will succeed. Principals must be aware of resistance to change, change models, and the impact of interaction between individuals and environment on implementation if change efforts are to be successful.

NOTES

Chin, R., & Benne, K. (1969). General strategies for effecting changes in human systems. In *The planning of change,* W. Bennis, et al., (eds.). New York: Holt, Rinehart, and Winston.

Hanson, M.E. (1991). *Educational administration and organizational behavior.* Boston: Allyn and Bacon.

Katz, D., & Kahn, R. (1966). *The social psychology of organizations.* New York: John Wiley.

National Association of Secondary School Principals. (1990). *Leader 1 2 3: Professional development program for school administrators.* Training manual. Reston, VA: NASSP.

Schmuck, R., & Runkel, P. (1988). *The handbook of organization development in schools.* Prospect Hills, IL: Waveland Press.

BIBLIOGRAPHY

109. Brandt, R. (1991). On local autonomy and school effectiveness: A
      conversation with John Chubb. *Educational Leadership, 48* (4), 57-
      60.
           Chubb states that the more influence principals have over
      personnel decisions, curriculum decisions, and restruction methods, the
      more effectively organized schools are likely to be. Further, Chubb
      advocates a public education system based on his research and market
      principles.

110. Chin, R., & Benne, K. (1969). General strategies for effecting
      changes in human systems. In *The planning of change,* W. Bennis
      et al., eds. New York: Holt, Rinehart, and Winston.
           This classic work on change details specific change models with
      rationale and implications for development.

111. Donmoyer, R., & Wagstaff, J.F. (1990). Principals can be
      effective managers and instructional leaders. *NASSP Bulletin, 74*
      (525), 20–25, 27, 29.
           The way in which principals perform their daily responsibilities
      and duties has a profound affect upon the faculty, staff, students, and the
      climate of the school. Guidelines for effective managers and instructional
      leaders are presented.

      Garten, T., & Valentine, J. Cited above as item 93.

112. Hanson, M.E. (1991). *Educational administration and
      organizational behavior.* Boston: Allyn and Bacon.
           This is a comprehensive overview of administrative behavior in
      schools. Of particular interest is the discussion of variables that impact
      the implementation of innovation in schools.

113. Katz, D., & Kahn R. (1966). *The social psychology of
      organizations.* New York: John Wiley.
           This classic work presents foundational aspects of human behavior
      in social organizations. The discussion of change in organizations is
      particularly useful in contemplating change in schools.

114. King, J. (1981). *Planning the elementary principal's year or an
      attempt to keep everyone happy. ACSA Operations Notebook 27.*
      Burlingame, CA: ACSA/Foundation for Educational

Administration. (ERIC Document Reproduction Service No. ED
239 358)

Operational guidelines for planning the school schedule are
provided in this 105-page manuscript sponsored by the Association of
California School Administrators. Contains strategies to effectively plan
the school schedule according to six administrative competencies:
instructional leadership, management, human relations, leadership,
political and cultural awareness, and self-awareness.

Lyons, J.E. Cited above as item 76.

National Association of Secondary School Principals. Cited above
as item 104.

115. Roitman, S. (1986). *ABCDF—Time management for new
administrators*. Paper presented at the 41st annual meeting of the
Association for Supervision and Curriculum Development, San
Francisco, CA. (ERIC Document Reproduction Service No. ED
270 863)

Administrators must learn to use their time wisely to be effective
managers. Strategies are provided which assist administrators in deciding
how to organize and prioritize their daily work responsibilities. Roitman
clearly identifies several time management techniques which facilitate the
accomplishment of objectives and tasks facing administrators.

Rogus, J.F. Cited above as item 80.

Rogus, J.F. Cited above as item 81.

Rutherford, W.L. Cited above as item 106.

Schmuck, R., & Runkel, P. Cited above as item 88.

Snyder, K.J. Cited above as item 108.

116. St. John, W. (1982). Effective planning, delegating, and priority
setting. *NASSP Bulletin, 66* (451), 16–24.

Provides administrators with information on how to increase
effectiveness in the time of declining resources as well as planning,
setting priorities, and delegating tasks.

CHAPTER 10

Delegation

INTRODUCTION

Delegation is an important leadership and management function of the principal. Delegation provides opportunities for principals to build greater school involvement by permitting decision making by those closest to the problems. In other respects, delegation allows for the division of labor and responsibility among school participants.

Delegation can be difficult for those leaders who believe that to get it done right, they have to do it themselves. Further, in delegating decisions, principals do give up some influence over decisions (Yukl, 1990). However, research does support the idea that teachers are more innovative and are willing to take more risks in school environments where key decisions are delegated to them by the principal (Short, Miller-Wood, & Johnson, 1991).

What Does It Mean to Delegate?

Delegation as a leadership and management function differs from participative decision making, a component of school restructuring and site-based management, in several ways. As mentioned earlier, delegation allows for the allocation of responsibilities among a number of school participants so that individuals do not become burdened excessively. Many times, those closest to the problem or highly invested in the activity may be better able to take responsibility for the outcome of decisions, freeing principals to work with other critical issues (Schmuck & Runkel, 1988; Yukl, 1990).

Delegation, does, however, provide opportunities, as with participative decision making, to develop the capacity of teachers to clarify problems, frame alternative solutions, and assume responsibility for outcomes. In addition, delegation can broaden the role of teachers, providing job enrichment and job satisfaction (Hughes & Ubben, 1984; Yukl, 1990).

As with participative decision making, delegation can foster commitment to and ownership of the school organization. Yukl (1990), however, suggests that delegation may not necessarily increase the quality of decisions, a benefit of shared decision making (Short & Greer, 1988). Rather, he suggests that delegation often results in expedient decisions, not quality decisions (Yukl, 1990).

What Are the Pitfalls of Delegating?

The pitfalls of delegation center on persons to whom the decisions and responsibilities are delegated. There is indication that some individuals prefer direction and structure in the work environment (Yukl, 1990). These persons, for whatever reason, do not desire additional responsibilities or authority. These may be teachers who feel overworked, stressed, or burned-out, or teachers who feel less competent than the principal to make decisions. Teachers may feel that they lack the time and resources to take on additional decision making roles in the school (Yukl, 1990; Short et al., 1991). Results of a national study of school empowerment indicated that some teachers actually feel that they do not know how to make good decisions (Short, Greer, & Michael, 1991). Though this may be surprising since teachers make many decisions in their classrooms during the course of the day, they feel less secure in a decision arena outside the classroom. However, few teachers or principals have been exposed to decision making or delegation training to increase their competence and confidence.

Are There Levels of Delegation?

Hughes and & Ubben (1984) suggest that there may be degrees of delegation. Degrees of delegation may depend on several issues: the ability of teachers, the nature of the decision or activity, and the general context of the school (Hughes & Ubben, 1984). Degrees of delegation involve several stages on a continuum, from asking a teacher to study an issue with the principal having final decision-making authority to telling the teacher to make the decision and take action (Hughes & Ubben, 1984). The impact of degrees of delegation on teachers may be to curtail teacher-risk taking and innovative activity (Short et al., 1991). Principals should be clear about the level of responsibility and authority that they are delegating to teachers.

What Are the Strategies for Delegating Effectively?

In contrast to considerations when forming problem solving groups in the school where issues of expertise and need for acceptance of the group decision are critical, principals face other concerns in delegating. These issues center on authority, understanding of role, monitoring, support, and autonomy.

Yukl (1990) suggests several points that relate to effective delegation: (1) determine how much authority is necessary; (2) insure teacher comprehension; (3) obtain teacher acceptance of responsibilities; (4) monitor teacher progress; (5) provide assistance and psychological support; and (6) discourage excessive dependence.

It appears that effective delegation requires the principal to communicate specifically the tasks and responsibilities required to carry out the activity or decision-making process. Teachers should understand clearly these expectations. The principal should discuss the amount of authority that the teachers will have as well as how the progress of the work will be monitored by the principal and teachers (Yukl, 1990).

A critical variable in effective delegation is participant buy-in to the effort. It is helpful to discuss and agree on goals, performance criteria, and time frames for completion (Yukl, 1990). Teachers should understand what types of resources will be available to them in carrying out the delegated tasks. The principal should establish a process to follow when encountering difficulties and problems (Yukl, 1990). Principals should avoid the tendency to step in and take over when problems arise. The principal, by delegating and avoiding the takeover, allows teachers to develop and grow as professionals (Hughes & Ubben, 1984).

Why Do Some Principals Fear Delegation?

Delegation may not come easy for some principals. Researchers have found that some principals have difficulty sharing power with teachers (Short et al., 1991). Principals fear losing control over the school (Yukl, 1990). Pressure on principals from the central office and the public force them to be sensitive to accountability issues which impede their inclination to delegate.

Some principals believe that teachers do not always make the best decisions (Short et al., 1991). Results of one study revealed that some principals are concerned about parent and community responses to poor decisions, decisions that are not in the best interest of kids, as one principal suggested (Short et al., 1991).

Delegation can be an important task of the principal which allows for development of teachers, the division of labor in accomplishing school goals and objectives, and building of commitment on the part of teachers to the school as an organization. There are critical issues in considering delegation and successful delegation requires attention to specific guidelines. Principals may have difficulty in delegating roles and responsibilities to teachers. Concerns about authority, control, and power may influence principal use of delegation.

NOTES

Hughes, L., & Ubben, G. (1984). *The elementary principal's handbook.* Boston: Allyn and Bacon.

Schmuck, R., & Runkel, P. (1988). *The handbook of organization development in schools.* Prospect Hills, IL: Waveland Press.

Short, P.M., & Greer, J.T. (1988, February). Shared governance: Impact on student outcomes. A paper presented at the annual meeting of the American Educational Research Association, San Francisco, CA.

Short, P.M., Greer, J.T., & Michael, R. (1991). Restructuring schools through empowerment: Facilitating the process. *Journal of School Leadership, 1* (2), 127-139.

Short, P.M., Miller-Wood, D.J., & Johnson, P.E. (1991). Risk taking and teacher involvement in decision making. *Education, 147* (1), 87-93.

Yukl, G.A. (1990). *Leadership in organizations.* Englewood Cliffs, NJ: Prentice-Hall.

BIBLIOGRAPHY

Cunard, R.F. Cited above as item 70.

117.   Currie, G., & Rhodes, J. (1991). Uncertainty and fragmentation: The "realities" of the principalship in the United States. (ERIC Document Reproduction Service No. ED 332 362)
Short-term planning is examined in this report, which also offers characteristics of the principal's work. Brevity, variety, interruption, uncertainty, and fragmentation emerged from the data regarding principals. Possible solutions include meaningful internships, local training programs, reflective evaluation, and continuous support.

Hughes. L., & Ubben, G. Cited above as item 100.

Leithwood, K.A., & Stager, M. Cited above as item 91.

Michael, S.R. Cited above as item 103.

Rees, R. Cited as item 105.

Rutherford, W.L. Cited above as item 106.

Schmuck, R., & Runkel, P. Cited above as item 88.

118.   Short, P.M., & Greer, J.T. (1988, February). Shared governance: Impact on student outcomes. Paper presented at the annual meeting of the American Educational Research Association, San Francisco, CA.
This paper presents a synthesis of research of participative decision making and its relationship to shared governance in schools. Strengths and weaknesses are discussed as they relate to increased teacher participation in school governance.

Short, P.M., Greer, J.T., & Michael, R. Cited above as item 44.

119.   Short, P.M., Miller-Wood, D.J., & Johnson, P.E. (1991). Risk taking and teacher involvement in decision making. *Education, 147* (1), 87-93.
Provides insight on principal facilitation of teacher risk taking.

St. John, W. Cited above as item 115.

120. Thomas, W. C. (1989). Delegation—A skill in school-based management. *NASSP Bulletin, 73* (518), 30–32.

An overview of the skills needed to delegate tasks and responsibilities in the school program. Specific procedures are provided for defining and delineating tasks, giving professionals the responsibility and authority for getting the job done, and giving credit to those fulfilling the tasks.

121. Weber, J.R. (1987). *Instructional leadership: Contexts and challenges.* (ERIC Document Reproduction Service No. ED 288 261)

The advantages of sharing instructional leadership responsibilities with school faculty in order to promote instructional programs and improve student performance are discussed. The qualities of effective leaders are discussed in terms of personal traits, their commitment to the school, and the management strategies employed.

Yukl, G.A. Cited above as item 84.

SECTION THREE
PROGRAMMATIC SKILLS

CHAPTER 11

Instructional Program

Principals are the key figures in the development of school instructional programs. As instructional leaders, principals must have a vision for improving the instructional program to meet the needs of all individuals. In regard to the instructional program, principals should consider the following: (1) visioning and empowering instructional programs for the improvement of teaching and learning; (2) recognizing the developmental needs of students; (3) insuring appropriate instructional experiences while accommodating differences in cognition and achievement; and (4) mobilizing the participation of appropriate people or groups to develop these programs and to establish a positive environment (Thomson, 1990).

THE GOALS OF INSTRUCTION

As education branches into many diverse areas, the educational leader of a school should seek to enhance the educational programs for both instructional and supplementary activities. Student success and ultimately principal success depends upon the special skills of the principal for adapting to the rapidly changing educational processes. School administrators must enhance their skills to recognize the developmental needs of students and new concepts in instructional methods (DeMoulin, 1991).

The developmental needs of children will escalate as society copes with poverty, drugs, abuse, and AIDS. Schools are often the only place of opportunity for these children to escape and to obtain the necessary life skills for success (Edelman, 1989). Only with positive experiences ensured by the principal can these opportunities for children become reality.

When a positive learning environment is present, instruction improves and learning is enhanced. The improvement of instruction and all other aspects of education depends upon the educational leader to provide for a positive learning environment. The use of available support personnel to enhance instruction should be considered by principals (Glickman & Pajak, 1989). Principals must work to get the most out of the school day for teachers, staff, and students. Student needs may be met by establishing expectations through a daily routine (Love, 1988).

To insure that appropriate instructional methods are used by teachers and support staff, the principal must be knowledgeable in teaching strategies and techniques. Active learning calls for student participation in the process of learning: students doing things. To provide the best learning opportunities, principals must be aware of the learning styles of students and the teaching styles of the teachers. The principal must be involved to assure that all children in all levels have learning opportunities. The educational leader must assist teachers and staff to focus on student learning and improved outcomes. Key elements of improved student learning identified by Blum and Kneidek (1991) are: focus on student performance, a strategic planning process, a data-driven process, and a research base.

THE SCHOOL OF THE FUTURE

Cawelti (1989) perceived four principles necessary to design the school of the future: (1) school organization, (2) curriculum, (3) staff development, and (4) technology. The school leader must collaborate with all individuals to achieve the appropriate design and instructional program for the school. Effective leaders realize that change and interactive instructional programs may create student anxiety, but then leaders are willing to take the risk to meet the diverse needs of children. The school principal must develop a vision for the school's instructional program and model the willingness to accomplish the vision.

New educational programs should assure both quality and efficiency, according to McGarry (1990). In implementing new instructional programs or changing existing ones, the principal should analyze the program based on cost, outcomes, changing personal and family needs, involvement of parents, collaboration among educators, and the results of research.

NEW INSTRUCTIONAL TECHNIQUES

To provide for the new concepts in instructional programs, the educational leader may have to implement a longer school day and/or school year (Love, 1988). Teaching partnerships and individualized student progress are also possibilities (DeMoulin, 1991). The involvement of teachers, staff, parents, and students in determining the instructional programs may also enhance the leadership of the school principal (Wallman, 1991). Effective schools research and school-based management may help the principal produce quality instructional programs (Thomson, 1991).

School success is based on a positive educational environment and the use of innovative programs for instructional purposes. New concepts mean new risks and increasing involvement. Change is based on political and economic necessities which include new directions for educating the children of poverty, identifying the disadvantaged learner, and accommodating the differences in student proficiency (Talleuico & Blumberg, 1991). Instructional programs must challenge students to reach beyond their intellectual grasp even if mistakes may occur (Weisglass, 1991).

Motivation will be a key component for the school leader to achieve an effective instructional program for the school. This may mean a dynamic change in the operation of the traditional school. Evans, Corsini, and Gazda (1990) state that "an untraditional school design based on democratic principles gives students control over their own learning and promotes the development of responsibility, respect, resourcefulness, and responsiveness" (52).

SUMMARY

Success for the unsuccessful is possible when educational programs involve teachers and students in selecting learning materials, decisions concerning use, and determining what results to expect. The school principal must be the motivator to assure that the instructional program involves the interaction of teachers and students to provide an effective learning opportunity.

NOTES

Blum, R.E. & Kneidek, A.W. (1991). Strategic improvement that focuses on student achievement. *Educational Leadership, 48* (7), 17–21.

Cawelti, G. (1989). Designing high schools for the future. *Educational Leadership, 47* (1), 30–35.

DeMoulin, D.F. (1991). School administration in the twenty-first century. *Journal of School Leadership, 1* (1), 54–58.

Edelman, M.W. (1989). Defending America's children. *Educational Leadership, 46* (8), 77–80.

Evans, T.D., Corsini, R.J., & Gazda, G.M. (1990). Individual education and the 4 Rs. *Educational Leadership, 48* (1), 52–56.

Glickman, C.D., & Pajak, E.F. (1989). Dimensions of school district improvement. *Educational Leadership, 46* (8), 61–64.

Love, I.H. (1988). Getting the most out of the school day. *Educational Leadership, 45* (7), 82.

McGarry, T.P. (1990). Chaos and opportunity. *Educational Leadership, 48* (3), 105.

National Commission for the Principalship. (1990). *Principals for our changing schools: Preparation and certification.* Fairfax, VA: National Commission for the Principalship.

Talleuico, M., & Blumberg, A. (1991). Instructional leadership in practice: Fostering meaningful exchange. *Journal of School Leadership, 1* (4), 316-327.

Thomson, S.D. (1991). Principals for America 2000. *Journal of School Leadership, 1* (4), 294-304.

Wallman, D.G. (1991). Relating theory to practice: Instructional leadership and the principal. *Journal of School Leadership, 1* (1), 87-90.

Weisglass, J. (1991). Teachers have feelings: What can we do about it. *Journal of Staff Development, 12* (1), 28-35.

BIBLIOGRAPHY

122. Anderson, L.W., & Pellicer, L.O. (1990). Synthesis of research on compensatory and remedial education. *Educational Leadership, 48* (1),10–16.
 Emphasizes using Chapter 1 programs with regular instructional programs to achieve student successes. The author points out that many programs do not provide for quality instruction because of teacher's aides and the fact that the children are often isolated at their own desks. Quality instruction must provide for adequate teaching and instructional programs.

123. ASCD Panel on Moral Education. (1988). Moral education in the life of the school. *Educational Leadership, 45* (9), 4–8.
 Human dignity is an important aspect in addressing the needs of today's children. Schools are given the burden of providing students the background for determining what is right or wrong. Instructional programs play an integral part in providing a successful scheme for addressing moral education. Commitment must come from both educators and parents working together as partners in providing moral education.

124. Becker, H.J. (1989). Using computers for instruction. *BYTE, 12* (2), 149–62.
 Reviews the results and implications of the 1985 National Survey of Instructional Uses of School Computers, a survey of elementary and secondary schools which examined teacher use as well as student use. Differences in student use are reported according to grade level, subject, ability level, and gender.

125. Benjamin, S. (1989). An ideascope for education: What futurists recommend. *Educational Leadership, 46* (1), 8–14.
 Futurists believe that global and multicultural pressures will show the path along which U.S. education will follow. Higher level thinking skills will become more necessary as life changes more rapidly and current knowledge will become obsolete quicker and people will need to be able to manage information and information systems more readily. More interaction with sources outside of the school environment will become the only way students will develop those skills necessary for survival.

126. Bennett, R.E. (1987). *Planning and evaluating computer education programs.* Columbus, OH: Merrill
 This book covers all areas of planning, implementing, and evaluating computer education programs for the school or school district.

Purposes of effective computer education programs are discussed along with proper software selection and effective evaluation. Includes computer education from a national perspective.

127. Bolanos, P.J. (1990). Restructuring the curriculum. *Principal, 69* (3), 13–14.

Discusses the Key School in Indianapolis, Indiana, which is a magnet school with a heterogeneous student body in a large, urban district. The school has drawn national attention for its collaborative, interdisciplinary curriculum development and alternative assessment methods. The instructional program involves central curricular themes to be continuously shaped by various interacting groups.

128. Blum, R.E., & Kneidek, A.W. (1991). Strategic improvement that focuses on student achievement. *Educational Leadership, 48* (7), 17–21.

Indicates how a school district became a pilot site for "Creating the Future," a research-based, district-level, strategic improvement process. The idea behind the process was to provide focus on student learning and improved outcomes. Several key elements are involved: focus on student performance, a strategic planning process, a data-driven process, and a research base.

129. Braddock, J.H. (1990). Tracking the middle grades: National patterns of group of instruction. *Phi Delta Kappan, 71* (6), 445–49.

This article presents current data from a 1988 Johns Hopkins University middle school survey on using between-class grouping and regrouping practices with early adolescents. Results from the survey indicate that learning opportunities in the middle grades remain highly stratified.

130. Campione, J.C. (1989). Assisted assessment: A taxonomy of approaches and an outline of strengths and weaknesses. *Journal of Learning Disabilities, 22* (3), 151–65.

This article reviews the criticisms of the traditional approaches to the assessment of student abilities and instructional program design and suggests dynamic new approaches. A major feature of these suggested approaches is assistance to influence student performance and thus reveal the potential for change. The approaches are categorized and examined according to their strengths and/or weaknesses.

131. Cawelti, G. (1989). Designing high schools for the future. *Educational Leadership, 47* (1), 30–35.

The article indicates that schools of the future should address four key principles: school organization, curriculum, staff development, and technology. Through collaboration of schools with other groups and agencies effective instructional programs may be developed.

132. Clabby, J.F., & Elias, M.J. (1988). Teaching social decision making. *Educational Leadership, 45* (7), 52–55.

Social decision making begins with social awareness that promotes standards for allowing individuals to make informed decisions which will affect their well-being. The following eight-step strategy has become quite effective in social decision making: (1) look for signs of different feelings, (2) acknowledge the problem, (3) choose a goal, (4) consider solutions, (5) analyze solutions separately, (6) choose best solution, (7) plan and make final check, and (8) try it and rethink it.

133. DeMoulin, D.F. (1991). School administration in the twenty-first century. *Journal of School Leadership, 1* (1), 54–58.

School administration has many different aspects to be considered as education branches out into so many diverse areas. Administrators attempt to direct each school-related activity to the best possible mode of success for all involved. As school environments, management techniques, and other educational processes rapidly change, so must the methods and styles of administering to those changes. Special skills will become necessary to adapt to the divergence of the school atmosphere. Administrators, as well as educators, will advance technologically or be left behind.

134. Edelman, M.W. (1989). Defending America's children. *Educational Leadership, 46* (8), 77–80.

Practical commitment to all our children should be the goal established by the nation as a whole. The unpleasant truths of abuse, poverty, and lack of parental support are just a few of the major problems facing our young people of today. Poverty levels of so many families leave them unable to provide the necessary developmental items and opportunities. As a result, our children fall so far behind that it is impossible for them to achieve much success. Schools must become stepping stones for the unfortunate children who lack the opportunity to attain life skills.

135. Glickman, C.D. & Pajak, E.F. (1989). Dimensions of school district improvement. *Educational Leadership, 46* (8), 61–64.

When a positive learning environment is presented, a better chance for improvement of instruction and other facets of education can be recognized and achieved. Support staff is essential for the quality of educational development to be maintained. Total commitment from faculty and administration is essential to provide the leadership for school improvement.

136. Hartley, E., & Wasson, E. (1989). An ounce of prevention . . . : A case study of a migrant gifted student. *Rural Special Education Quarterly, 10* (1), 26–30.

The article examines a multi-criteria assessment program for the identification of gifted minority students in a small rural Washington school district. It relates the case study of the gifted at-risk migrant student with limited English proficiency.

137. Hillerich, R.L. (1990). What does "grade level" mean? *Principal, 69* (3), 47–48.

Attempts to define what is meant by educators when we refer to grade level. Grade level is defined as an age grouping that yields an achievement distribution approximating a normal curve, with the distribution average at grade level in a typical school. It suggests that with an average teacher, an average child gains one year, and that educators must accept this normal range of reading achievement and adjust instruction accordingly.

138. Joyce, B. (1990). *Changing school culture through staff development.* Alexandria, VA: Association for Supervision and Curriculum Development.

Offers insight on improving our schools through the proper use of staff development. The principal's role in teacher development, and staff development and the restructured school are two important areas discussed. The book includes information from current studies in Pittsburgh, Los Angeles, and Lincoln, Nebraska.

139. Link, F. (1985). *Essays on the intellect.* Alexandria, VA: Association for Supervision and Curriculum Development.

Essay topics include intellectual development of the gifted, strategy for intellectual and academic improvement, and development of intellectual capability.

140. Love, I.H. (1988). Getting the most out of the school day. *Educational Leadership, 45* (6), 82.

Provides an insight into the use of daily training to gain valuable time in the classroom routine. The use of time schedules for events and educational opportunity enhances the positive environment of the educational process. The use of daily projects for students develops the expectations and successes for those involved.

141.   McGarry, T.P. (1990). Chaos and opportunity. *Educational Leadership, 48* (3), 105.

The author states that a new educational program should assure both quality and efficiency. Criteria to consider for instructional programs include that they (1) be cost effective, (2) be outcome-based, (3) address changing personal and family needs, (4) professionalize staff, (5) involve parents, (6) foster collaboration among educators, and (7) conduct ongoing research. With education reform and the changing global society, school leaders must address the concepts of providing effective instructional program.

142.   Sclafani, S. & Smith, R.A. (1989). Integrated teaching systems: Guidelines for evaluation. *Computing Teacher, 17* (3), 36–38.

Describes integrated teaching systems (ITS) and discusses guidelines to be considered when purchasing and implementing such a system. Topics discussed include instructional theories, appropriate grade levels and curriculum areas, management and reporting systems, and cost considerations.

143.   Shane, H.G. (1989). Educated foresight for the 1990's. *Educational Leadership, 47* (1), 4–6.

Identifies the need to change the school year and school day. The emphasis is on addressing the needs of students, faculty, staff, and administration for succeeding at achieving student progress. Teaching partnerships may be necessary.

144.   Strother, D.B. (1990). Building exemplary schools. *Phi Delta Kappan, 72* (4), 323–326.

The author indicates the need to use school-site management in building exemplary schools. Other facets include outcome-based assessments and widespread community involvement. Instructional programs should be structured to provide more authority and flexibility at the school level under the leadership of the school principal which requires a highly competent and well-organized administrator at the building-level.

CHAPTER 12
Curriculum Design

An effective school curriculum is based on research, experience, and teaching methodology. As instructional leader of the school, the principal is a critical element in curriculum development. McCauley (1990) identifies several skills a principal should possess in order to work effectively with faculty to determine the curriculum of the school.

WHAT IS CURRICULUM?

Curriculum has been defined in various ways: as a plan, as experience, as a field of study and in subject matter and grade level terms (Lunenberg & Ornstein, 1991). A broad definition implies experience at several levels: curriculum is the plan (what is to be taught), the instruction (what is actually taught), the outcomes (what was evaluated), and the teaching techniques (how it was taught). Although some principals would disagree with this definition, most administrators rely on Dewey's "experience and education" definition of curriculum (Dewey, 1938), or Caswell and Campbell's (1935) belief that curriculum is "all the experiences children have under the guidance of the teacher" (p. 69). Knegevich (1984) states that "curriculum refers to all the educational experiences provided under the auspices of a school" (p. 422).

121

Curriculum Development

Lunenberg and Ornstein (1991) outline three steps in curriculum development: (1) planning a curriculum, (2) implementing the curriculum, and (3) evaluating the curriculum. Under ideal conditions, those people affected by curriculum development—administrators, supervisors, teachers, students, parents, community, and principals—should be involved in each of the three steps in the process. Without ownership of the curriculum, those affected will often sabotage the best "plans" for curriculum development. Whether overtly or covertly, teachers can effectively stifle any curriculum change.

Basic Approaches to Curriculum Development

Lunenberg and Ornstein (1991) specify four basic approaches to curriculum development: (1) behavioral, (2) managerial, (3) systematic, and (4) humanistic. They further contend that curriculum development is "largely a function of leadership style and involves personal interaction, program development, and organizational structure" (Lunenberg & Ornstein, 1991, p. 416).

SKILLS NEEDED BY PRINCIPALS

Key skills needed by principals involved in curriculum development have been identified by the National Commission for the Principal (1990). These skills include: (1) interpreting school district curricula; (2) planning and implementing with staff a framework for instruction; (3) initiating needs analyses; (4) monitoring social and technological developments as they affect curriculum; (5) responding to international content levels; and (6) adjusting content as needs and conditions change.

WHAT IS THE ROLE OF THE PRINCIPAL?

Research supports the assumption that principals should interpret the curriculum for the school as specified by school district policies and state regulations. Curriculum leadership is necessary to determine the framework for instruction. Education reform and school-based decision making enhances the chances for faculty involvement in planning and implementing a curriculum framework.

Cetron (1990) speculates that a key role of the school principal is providing leadership for developing a curriculum to meet the needs of all students. Brandt (1990) suggests that school restructuring will place new demands on school administrators to develop a dynamic curriculum to meet the needs of students. Tye (1991) reports that as the world constantly changes, educational leaders must initiate a systematic analysis to determine curriculum needs for a global society. As technology changes, the principal must be aware of social and technological developments as they relate to curriculum development. Technology in the classroom and new delivery methods are essential to enhancing the curriculum and improving student achievement.

Principals should address the needs of students based on research, needs analyses, reform mandates, and changes in society. The principal is a primary force affecting the curriculum. Effective curriculum development initiatives should focus on student outcomes. Principals must have strong interpersonal skills for involving others in curriculum development.

Change as a Function of Curriculum Development

The school principal must have a clear vision, commitment to curriculum development, and be a risk taker in order to implement curriculum change. The principal should share decision making with faculty and community to implement changes in curriculum design. English (1986) specified that the principal is critical to developing, implementing, and monitoring the curricula of the school. All principals must consider the values and complexities of the community as they work with others to design and implement curricula for twenty-first century schools.

NOTES

Brandt, R.S. (1990). Restructuring: Where is it? *Educational Leadership, 47* (7), 3.

Caswell, H.L., & Campbell, D.S. (1935). *Curriculum development.* New York: American Books.

Cetron, M.J. (1990). *Educational renaissance.* New York: St. Martin's Press.

Dewey, J. (1938). *Experience and education.* New York: Macmillan.

English, F.W. (1986). Who is in charge of the curriculum? In T. Koerner's *Rethinking reform: The principal's dilemma.* Reston, VA: National Association of Secondary School Principals.

Knezevich, S.J. (1984). *Administration of public education.* (4th Ed.). New York: Harper & Row.

Lunenberg, F.C., & Ornstein, A.C. (1991). *Educational administration: Concepts and practices.* Belmont, CA: Wadsworth.

McCauley, C.D. (1990). *Effective school principals: Competencies for meeting the demands of educational reform.* Greensboro, NC: Center for Creative Leadership.

National Commission for the Principalship. (1990). *Principals for our changing schools: Preparation and certification.* Fairfax, VA: National Commission for the Principalship.

Tye, K.A. (1991). Introduction: The world at a crossroads. In *Global education: From thought to action.* The 1991 ASCD Yearbook. Alexandria, VA: Association for Supervision and Curriculum Development.

BIBLIOGRAPHY

145. Aronstein, L.W., & DeBenedictis, K.L. (1988). The principal as a leader of curriculum change: A study of exemplary school administrators. (ERIC document Reproduction Service No. ED 296 481)

A study conducted in Massachusetts between October 1986 and May 1987 assessed the behaviors and skills principals exhibit when they make curricular revision. Actual curriculum development meetings between principals and teachers were observed. The principals were observed to use two types of strategies; one strategy stressed curriculum development, and the other emphasized enabling actions.

Ashbaugh, C.R., & Kasten, K.L. Cited above as item 49.

146. Bailey, G.D. (1990). How to improve curriculum leadership—twelve tenets. Tips for principals from NASSP. (ERIC Document Reproduction Service No. ED 315 905).

Twelve basic tenets can be used to guide administrators who want to become effective curriculum leaders. These represent different ways of looking at curriculum leadership and include: curriculum leaders see curriculum development as a continuous process, they see the interconnectedness of curriculum supervision and staff development, and they operate as facilitators and seek consensus rather than compromise.

147. Becker, J. (1991). Curriculum consideration in global studies. In K.A. Tye's *Global education: From thought to action.* 1991 Yearbook of the Association for Supervision and Curriculum Development. Alexandria, VA: Association for Supervision and Curriculum Development, 67–85.

Emphasizes global studies in the curriculum to address the new state of the world affairs. With the new global community educational leaders should make curriculum decisions to address these global changes. Reform and curricula with a global perspective are necessary for addressing the changing global society.

148. Blank, R.K. (1987). The role of principal as leader: Analysis of variation in leadership of urban high schools. *The Journal of Educational Research, 81* (2), 69–79.

Identifies the role of the principal as the instructional leader and relates research on the principal's leadership capacity and skills. The emphasis is on the relationship between the principal and the curriculum.

Principals should lead instructional improvement and innovation and involve others in making curriculum changes.

149. Brandt, R.S. (Ed. (1988). *Content of the curriculum.* 1988 ASCD Yearbook of the Association for Supervision and Curriculum Development. Alexandria, VA: ASCD.

This book provides an overview of the content of the curriculum for schools. A key component relates to what schools should teach in regard to social studies, English, science, mathematics, and foreign languages. Other curriculum areas addressed include health education, physical education, fine arts, and technology. Educational leaders should carefully consider the content of the curriculum based on research and the needs of the children.

150. Cetron, M.J. (1989). Class of 2000. *The School Administrator, 46* (2), 8–11.

The author asks questions concerning the future of curriculum and education for the students of the class of 2000. Emphasis is given to a need to enhance the curriculum to meet the needs of a changing society. Educational reform must address the new technology, develop a modern curriculum, and prepare students to perform in new roles in society and the work force.

151. Cetron, M.J. (1990). *Educational renaissance.* New York: St. Martin's Press.

Provides theoretical concepts of the need for addressing education's critical trends for the future. Curriculum and instruction are major areas of concern. Leadership from the principal has an impact on curriculum decisions regarding school reform and a changing society. Emphasis is given to providing a curriculum which is connected to jobs and work.

152. Chopra, R.K. (1989). Synergistic curriculum development: An idea whose time has come. *NASSP Bulletin, 73* (518), 44-50.

Describes a Kansas public school district's efforts to develop a synergistic curriculum plan combining the most positive elements of a standardized curriculum with those of a school-based curriculum. Encouraging staff commitment demands mutuality of expectation, dependence, trust, respect, communication, and vision.

153. Coble, L.D. (1989). Curriculum audits benefit strong, weak districts. *The School Administrator, 46* (10), 19–21.

Provides insight into using the curriculum audit concept to develop strategic planning to enhance curriculum and instruction. The emphasis of the article is on the curriculum audit process and how curriculum equity is determined. From the curriculum audit districts and educational leaders may make decisions to implement change or enhance the curriculum through strategic planning.

154. Cronin, H., Meadows, D., & Sinatra, R. (1990). Integrating computers, reading, and writing across the curriculum. *Educational Leadership, 48* (1), 57–62.

Identifies the key factor for the successful integration of computer instruction. Teachers and students perform curriculum mapping to assist in curriculum development. The concepts of technology and curriculum are a major component of the changing curriculum for schools.

155. Dede, C. (1989). The evolution of information technology: Implications for curriculum. *Educational Leadership, 46* (1), 23–26.

Assessment methods evaluate student attainment of higher-order skills. Computer-supported collaborative learning will become a major type of student interaction. Curriculum emphasis will shift from acquiring data to discussing ideas.

156. English, F.W. (1988). *Curriculum auditing.* Lancaster, PA: Technomic Publishing Co.

Identifies the concepts and principles instructional leaders should use in determining the effectiveness of the curriculum of both the school and school district. Curriculum auditing is a process which may be used to identify the key strengths and weaknesses of the school's curriculum. The team approach for analysis assists an educational leader in determining steps and procedures to enhance the current curriculum.

English, F.W., & Hill, J.C. Cited above as item 31.

157. Erlandson, D., & Schoenfeldt, L. (1989). *The management profile: A handbook for the development of management skills.* College Station, TX: Texas A & M University.

The concepts identified by the authors provide a process for assessing educational leaders regarding their management skills, including curriculum management. Curriculum management is a key function for the educational leader. This volume addresses how the principal can implement changes to improve the curriculum. Skills required to be an effective school manager are identified in the book.

158. Farrell, G.E. (1989). Curriculum development, implementation, and evaluation: A cross-cultural study of secondary schools in Australia, Canada, England, and the State of Georgia. (ERIC Document Reproduction No. ED 307 326)

Curriculum processes in representative areas of four large Western countries are investigated. Core curricula in these countries are markedly similar. Results indicate some confusion among school leaders on responsibilities for curriculum decisions, along with a desire to include a variety of constituencies in the processes. Teacher involvement was particularly emphasized across countries. Each group of principals acknowledged that massive curriculum development or revision was underway due to centralized mandates.

159. Gehlbach, R.D. (1990). Art education: Issues in curriculum and research. *Educational Researcher, 19* (7), 19–25.

This article defines the problem of fine arts not being emphasized in the curriculum of most public schools. Criteria for defining the art education curriculum are identified. The author encourages instructional leaders to look at the positive implications for students when art education curriculum is included in the school's curriculum.

160. Hill, J.C. (1990). The principal as curriculum supervisor. *Principal, 69* (3), 6-9.

Principals can improve their approach to curriculum supervision by applying six supervisory processes (organizing, planning, coping with change, implementing, problem solving, and evaluating) to six curriculum levels (written, taught, resourced, experienced, tested, and ideal) and using three supervisory roles (as monitor, standard-bearer, and first teacher).

161. Hord, S.M., & Huling-Austin, L. (1987). Curriculum implementation: How to know if it's there (or not there). *Journal of Rural and Small Schools, 1* (3), 23-26.

Provides and describes an Innovation Configuration checklist and how it was used by one rural principal to support teachers as they implemented a new math curriculum. The article also notes the significant role of leadership team and outlines seven principles of curriculum implementation.

162. Hunkins, F.P., & Ornstein, A.C. (1988) A challenge for principals—Designing the curriculum. *NASSP Bulletin, 72* (509), 50-59.

To help educators design a balanced curriculum giving students opportunities to master knowledge and use it appropriately, this article explains curriculum design components and framework and provides advice concerning selecting the design, exploring sources, working with the committee, and developing guiding statements.

163. Kanpol, B., & Weisz, E. (1990). The effective principal and curriculum—A focus on leadership. *NASSP Bulletin, 74* (525), 15-18.

The effective leadership literature fails to present a clear understanding of the principal's relationship to the curriculum. Principals must understand the enacted curriculum process, not just the official curriculum. Trust, open dialogue, a collaborative support system, and tolerance are essential ingredients to curriculum development and implementation.

164. Liston, D.P. & Zeichner, K.M. (1990). Teacher education and the social context of schooling: Issues for curriculum development. *American Educational Research Journal, 27* (4), 610–636.

This article provides concepts to be considered by educational leaders in developing curricula. When developing curricula, principals should consider social, political, and the institutional contexts of schooling. The rationale for an effective curriculum agenda is discussed relating to: (1) teachers' work, (2) minority cultures and majority schooling, and (3) gender and teaching. Emphasis is placed on changes needed in teacher preparation programs.

165. Mamchur, C. (1990). But . . . the curriculum. *Phi Delta Kappan, 71* (8), 634–637.

Considers ten questions regarding the effectiveness of the curriculum and student achievement. Principals should be aware of the concepts of curriculum and how effectively the curriculum is designed to meet the individual needs of students. Involvement of students in determining the curriculum may be a concept principals can use in enhancing the effectiveness of the school curriculum.

166. Miller, R.D. (Ed). (1988). *Challenges for school leaders.* Arlington, VA: American Association of School Administrators.

Includes information on the importance of curriculum leadership and the decision making processes school leaders use in curriculum development. School reform often mandates curriculum reform. School administrators have the greatest opportunity to impact curriculum development. Data from a research survey identify the concepts an effective curriculum should consider. The school leader must have a strong vision and commitment to curriculum development.

167. Murphy, J. (1990). Instructional leadership: Focus on curriculum responsibilities. *NASSP Bulletin, 74* (525), 1-4.

Principals must attend to eight curricular issues in their role as instructional leaders: (1) amount of content, (2) extent of academic focus on course work, (3) focus and sequence of courses, (4) breadth versus depth of content, (5) differential access to knowledge, (6) homework as an extension of content, (7) curricular alignment, and (8) quality of course objectives.

168. Murphy, J. (1990). Principal instructional leadership. In L. S. Lotto & P. W. Thruston, eds., *Recent advances in educational administration.* Greenwich, CT: JAI Press.

Identifies the role and skills principals should have regarding instructional leadership. Emphasis is on the curriculum and development of faculty for effective educational processes. The concepts and skills principals should develop regarding instructional leadership are related to the advances which are occurring in educational administration.

169. Smith, W.F., & Andrews, R.L. (1989). *Instructional leadership: How principals make a difference.* Alexandria, VA: Association for Supervision and Curriculum Development.

Identifies the role of the principal as the instructional leader. The skills and role expectations for a principal to be effective are discussed, including the use of a clinical supervision model to assure effective delivery of the curriculum. Issues are discussed that relate to the importance of how curriculum is developed and who makes the decisions.

170. Short, P., & Spencer W. (1990). Principal instructional leadership. *Journal of Research and Development in Education, 23* (2), 117–122.

Provides research data on the role of principals as instructional leaders. Data comes from students, teachers and principals. The skills and roles principals perform as instructional leaders are directly related to the curriculum of a school. Principals are a key component for determining the curriculum of the school and should use effective research to justify their role.

171. VanTassel-Baska, J. (1989). Appropriate curriculum for gifted learners. *Educational Leadership, 46* (6), 13–15.

This article provides instructional leaders elements to consider in developing curriculum for gifted learners. The process could be used for any curriculum component. An appropriate curriculum must have effective planning and include the following: (1) curriculum, (2) instruction, and (3) materials adapted to the learners involved.

CHAPTER 13

Student Guidance and Development

In today's schools, student guidance and development are important components of the educational process. The principal's role is to assure that the programs in these areas meet the needs of the students and promote student growth and development through providing the auxiliary services to support the programs. Kimbrough and Burkett (1990) have identified several areas principals should address in the area of student guidance and development including: (1) providing for student guidance, counseling, and auxiliary services; (2) utilizing community organizations; (3) responding to family needs; (4) enlisting the participation of appropriate people and groups to design and conduct these programs; (5) connecting schooling with plans for adult life; and (6) planning for a comprehensive program of student activities.

GUIDING STUDENTS FOR LIFE EXPERIENCES

In providing student guidance, counseling, and auxiliary services, principals should establish programs to meet the needs of the student. With the number of challenges and temptations that students face from drug and alcohol abuse, the competition for job placements, and college admission requirements, an effective guidance and counseling program is essential to assist students to determine the best choices for success (Geltner & Shelton, 1991). Guidance programs are not simply a scheduling phenomena but represent an attempt by the school to provide consultation to students as they determine their future role in life.

USING COMMUNITY AGENCIES

Principals should utilize community organizations, civic service functions, and public social service agencies to provide assistance to students in areas where funds or services are not available. With the number of homeless students, child abuse cases, poverty, and at-risk cases, principals must develop effective collaborative structures with the social service agencies to provide services for these students. The student guidance and development program cannot always provide adequate services in all these areas due to limited funding and staffing (Gorton & Ohlemacher, 1987).

MEETING FAMILY NEEDS

The contemporary American family depends upon the school for many services and often calls on the principal to assist or to respond to family needs. The principal must provide the guidance and counseling services required to assist these families which may require special programs for health, counseling, or consultation services (Remley & Albright, 1988).

STUDENT ACTIVITIES

The effective principal must plan a comprehensive co-curricular program for student activities. This can best be accomplished through the involvement of people and groups who will utilize these programs. As student activity programs are generated to support the educational objectives of the school and to provide the special services for guidance and development of students, they should support adult life and life-long learning. New technology will generate many demands on members of society, therefore students must be provided the skills for life-long learning and for planning for the future.

SUMMARY

The student guidance and development program should assist all students in developing skills to be caring and sharing members of society. The role of the principal is to assist in seeing that these programs are developed and implemented.

NOTES

Geltner, B.B., & Shelton, M.M. (1991). Expanded notions of strategic instructional leadership: The principal's role with student support personnel. *Journal of School Leadership, 1* (4), 338-350.

Gorton, R.G., & Ohlemacher, R. (1987). Counselor evaluation: A new priority for the principal's agenda. *NASSP Bulletin, 71* (496), 120-124.

Kimbrough, R.B., & Burkett, C.W. (1990). *The principalship: concepts and practices.* Englewood Cliffs, NJ: Prentice-Hall.

Remley, T.P, Jr., & Albright, P.L. (1988). Expectations for middle school counselors: views of students, teachers, principals, and parents. *The School Counselor, 35* (4), 290-296.

BIBLIOGRAPHY

172. Baron, J., & Brown, R.V. (1991). *Teaching decision making to adolescents.* Hillsdale, NJ: Lawrence Erlbaum Associates, Inc.

Provides the concepts for a variety of programs based on psychological theory and modern decision analysis designed to teach adolescents how to improve both their own decision making skills and their understanding of the decision making of others. Advice and theoretical concepts relate to the relevant need to address adolescent problems, especially drug abuse.

173. Bornstein, M.H., (Ed.) (1991). *Cultural approaches to parenting.* Hillsdale, NJ: Lawrence Erlbaum Associates, Inc.

Discusses the similarities and differences in enculturation processes that help to account for the ways in which individuals in different cultures develop. The concepts address different cross-cultural results from parenting. Specific areas of study include environment and interactive style, responsiveness, activity patterns and development of the social self.

174. Bryant, B.J. (1991). Getting the most from your school counseling program. *NASSP Bulletin, 75,* (535), 1–4.

Describes the three basic area needs to fully develop a quality school counseling program: counseling, consulting, and coordinating. These helpful processes usually allow maintenance of counselors' duties to be as productive as possible. Counseling develops individual as well as group programs which hopefully initiate trust and some confidentiality between group members. Consultation allows for thought processes to provide alleviation of some problems and coordination provides organization of necessary life skills programs.

175. Cantor, J.A. (1990). Job training and economic development initiatives: A study of potentially useful companions. *Educational Evaluation and Policy Analysis, 12* (2), 121–138.

Discusses a research study on information regarding job training and economic development through interorganizational collaboration. Utilizing educational components and businesses the study focused on innovative job creation practices. What works and why were analytically assessed.

176. Gage, N.L. (1990). Dealing with the dropout problem. *Phi Delta Kappan, 72* (4), 280–285.

Discusses the importance of dealing with the dropout problem as related to the national goal of increasing high school graduation rate to 90 percent by the year 2000. Emphasis is given to improving current dropout prevention programs through research and development. Involving parents and counseling in these programs is a major factor in providing students with the ability to succeed and graduate.

177. Gal, M.D., Gall, J.P., Jacobsen, D.R., & Bullock, T.L. (1990). *Tools for learning: A guide to teaching study skills.* Alexandria, VA: Association for Supervision and Curriculum Development.

Describes the concepts for teaching effective study skills to students, developing self-management skills, and developing self esteem. The ability to use the tools for learning is a facet principals should address in meeting the individual needs of students.

178. Gonzalez, M.L. (1990). School + home = a program for educating homeless students. *Phi Delta Kappan, 71* (10), 785–787.

Emphasizes what schools may do to meet the needs of the children utilizing a home concept at the school. The increasing number of homeless students adds merit to the program described. Emphasis is on providing a climate of sharing, caring, and learning for the children.

179. Hanson, J.R. (1988). Learning styles, visual literacies, and a framework for reading instruction. *Reading Psychology, 9* (4), 409–30.

Argues that reading instruction should be understood as an integrated instructional program alongside learning styles, modality dependencies, and visual literacies. Also indicates that teaching the "basics" of reading includes mastery of the fundamentals leading to verbal interaction, critical reading, and synthesis which produce creative reading and writing.

180. Hawley, R.A. (1990). The bumpy road to drug-free schools. *Phi Delta Kappan, 72* (4), 310–314.

Discusses the steps for national action to produce drug-free schools as based on the national education goal. Historically, drug use has had a major impact on school-age children. Special programs at the public schools for counseling and support are essential for reducing drug use. Emphasizes that it will not be an easy task and will require many individuals: educators, parents, students, civic groups, and public agencies.

181. Kataoka, T. (1985). *The influence of class management and student guidance upon academic work at the elementary and lower secondary education levels in Japan.* Washington: United States

Government. (ERIC Document Reproduction Service No. ED 271 397)

An important aspect of Japanese schooling is the attention given to class management and student guidance. The Japanese school curriculum for the elementary and the lower secondary school consists of three areas: (1) regular subjects; (2) moral education; and (3) special activities. Successes and concerns associated with the class management and student guidance program are discussed.

182. Kohn, A. (1990). Caring kids: The role of the schools. *Phi Delta Kappan, 72* (7), 496–506.

Provides a detailed insight into how psychological research, common sense, and the experiences of individuals should be used to help children grow into caring adults. Emphasis is on problem children and how schools should provide special programs to assist these children to care about others through positive actions. Learning through an innovative process which helps children become caring and responsible provides for the development of social values in the individuals.

183. Lake, S. (1988). *Scheduling in the middle level school: Philosophy into practice.* Sacramento: California League of Middle schools. (ERIC Document Reproduction Service No. ED 300 920)

Discusses the goals of using a "core block" curriculum to improve the overall program at the middle school level. The seven goals include (1) transition; (2) student guidance; (3) belonging; (4) interdisciplinary focus; (5) teacher collegiality and professionalism; (6) variety of instructional methods; and (7) access to key learning experiences. The "house" plan described is viewed as a possible bridge from the self-contained elementary classroom to the multi-teacher, departmentalized mode of high school.

Link, F. Cited above as item 139.

184. Marsh, H.W., & Holmes, L.W.M. (1990). Multidimensional self-concepts: Construct validation of responses by children. *American Educational Research Journal, 27* (1), 89–117.

Describes the research on self-concept and the use of multidimensional facets in instruments. Emphasis is on how different instruments might be used to relate and validate responses by children. Educators should be aware of the self-concepts of children regarding achievement and assessment processes.

185. McLaughlin, M.W., & Talbert, J. (1990). Constructing a personalized school environment. *Phi Delta Kappan, 72* (3), 230–235.

Describes how a personalized school environment is the product of strategic choices about organizational structures and routines. In these schools, teachers have a broader role with personalized instructional strategies. A special staff of counselors and aides is in constant touch with students' families. The interaction provides success for students and the family.

186. Medway, F.J., & Cafferty, T.P. (Eds.). (1991). *School psychology: A social psychological perspective.* Hillsdale, NJ: Lawrence Erlbaum Associates, Inc.

Covers the basics on school psychology and social psychology. The concept of combining these areas is discussed in terms of specific educational and social problems such as substance abuse, loneliness, and integration. With students facing major emotional problems, educators should be aware of the major components of school and social psychology.

187. Mikulecky, L. (1990). National adult literacy and lifelong learning goals. *Phi Delta Kappan, 72* (4), 304–309.

Addresses the adult literacy problem and work in the public schools to develop lifelong learning goals. Given the national educational goals of eliminating illiteracy, educators are challenged to promote the development of lifelong learning goals in students. Needs to be addressed are minority enrollment and counseling programs to encourage effective activities for all students.

188. Pogrow, S. (1990). Challenging at-risk students: Findings from the HOTS program. *Phi Delta Kappan, 71* (5), 389–397.

Describes research and the impact the HOTS program has had on at-risk students. Emphasizes that education can provide sophisticated interventions to enhance the learning of at-risk students. A key component is to establish expectations and provide rewards for those students who develop through the program. Principals are essential to the development and implementation of such programs.

189. Reed, S., & Saautter, R.C. (1990). Children of poverty: The status of 12 million young Americans. *Phi Delta Kappan, 71* (10), K1–K12.

This special report describes the impact poverty has on over twelve million children in America. What education should be doing to address the needs of the at-risk children is discussed. It is important that educators understand the cultural background of children. The emphasis on schools as social centers provides several methods of addressing these issues.

190. Schunk, D.H. (1991). *Learning theories: An educational perspective.* New York: Macmillan.
    Details each of the different learning theories which have been used in education throughout its history and gives insight into the men who gave life to such theories. Giants in the field of psychology such as Skinner, Piaget, and Thorndike are profiled to provide an appropriate understanding of how these theories originated and how they might be used by the practicing educator today.

191. Speece, D.L., & Cooper, D.H. (1990). Ontogeny of school failure: Classification of first-grade children. *American Educational Research Journal, 27* (1), 119–140.
    The conclusion of this research is that by capturing the variability of skills across clusters of children educators may design interventions that ameliorate the risk of failure for some groups of children.

192. Stern, D., Dayton, C., Paik, I., & Weisberg, A. (1989). Benefits and costs of dropout prevention in a high school program combining academic and vocational education: Third-year results from replications of the California peninsula academies. *Educational Evaluation and Policy Analysis, 11* (4), 405–416.
    Reports the research results from an evaluation of academy programs and high schools in California. The emphasis was on dropout prevention and how the grade level cohorts saved students from becoming dropouts. Data was identified on the cost and economic benefits to society of the programs provided.

193. Ullrich, T. (1989). Who are the "gifted"? *Curriculum in context: Journal of the Washington State Association for Supervision and Curriculum Development, 17* (1), 14–15.
    Addresses the question that many educators find hard to answer: "Who are the gifted?" Indicates that six criteria should be used in determining the truly gifted: (1) academic ability, (2) general intellectual ability, (3) creative talent, (4) leadership, (5) visual or performing arts, and (6) psychomotor skills.

CHAPTER 14

Staff Development

The principal has a major role in determining the direction for development of all faculty and staff. According to the guidelines of the National Commission for the Principalship (Thomson, 1990), the principal should be involved in the following activities as related to staff development: (1) identifying with participants the professional needs of individuals and groups; (2) planning and organizing programs to improve staff effectiveness; (3) supervising individuals and groups; (4) engaging staff and others to plan and participate in recruitment and development; (5) initiating self-development.

ESTABLISHING A STAFF DEVELOPMENT PLAN

With human resource development as a goal, the principal should work with school participants to establish a staff development system which ensures that all education personnel are in a continuous state of professional growth. A proposed staff development system should provide service to individuals, the school, and district-sponsored initiatives for school improvement. The principal, as instructional leader, should collaborate with faculty and staff for planning and organizing programs to improve staff participation and support (Keedy & Rogers, 1991).

ADULT LEARNING

Staff development effectiveness is based on the condition of the school and those designated to generate effective curriculum and instruction for the school. The creation of an environment and climate conducive to staff development is critical. Programs should be developed by those who will participate in the activities and should be related to research on adult learning. Educators acquire new skills and strategies utilizing the concepts of andragogy, or how adults learn (Richardson, Flanigan, & Prickett, 1991). The goals of staff development should be integrated to provide opportunities for individuals, small groups, large groups, and entire staffs to participate in the learning opportunities (Usher, 1987).

EVALUATING STAFF DEVELOPMENT

Staff development programs also must have an evaluation process to determine effectiveness and identify strengths and weaknesses. Evaluation of staff development programs allows principals to enhance or improve staff development opportunities. The evaluation process involves teacher and principal documentation and a review of available data to determine effectiveness. Logically, the behaviors of teachers, staff, and administrators involved in staff development should reflect the programs and growth opportunities provided.

IMPLEMENTATION

There are many different types of staff development programs which require minimal costs to implement. Many programs may be supported through local personnel who have expertise in many of the program areas or who may receive special training and provide training for trainers. A variety of methods for providing faculty release time for participation in staff development are available. Often, the only limitation is the creativity and ingenuity of the principal to design ways for faculty and staff to grow through activities.

SUMMARY

An integrated staff development program for all personnel provides opportunities to benefit from each other and can assure life-long learning.

An effective staff development program must be developed within the policies and regulations of the school and school district and function within the fiscal resources available. Principals must use innovation and creativity in developing these effective programs.

NOTES

Keedy, J.L., & Rogers, K. (1991). Teacher collegial groups: A structure for promoting professional dialogue conducive to organizational change. *Journal of School Leadership, 1* (1), 65–73.

Richardson, M.D., Flanigan, J.L., & Prickett, R.L. (1991). Adult learning theory: Implications for teachers of adults. *Indian Journal of Adult Education, 52* (1), 22–27.

Thomson, S.D. (1990). *Principals for our changing schools: Preparation and certification.* Fairfax, VA: National Commission on the Principalship.

Usher, R.S. (1987). The place of theory in designing curricula for the continuing education of adult educators. *Studies in the Education of Adults, 19* (1), 26–35.

BIBLIOGRAPHY

194. Bell, B. (Ed.). (1990). AASA cites five districts for professional development. *The School Administrator, 47* (7), 24–25.

Describes five different professional development programs used by school districts across the United States. These five districts were presented awards by the American Association of School Administrators for their effectiveness in professional development within the districts. One district established an instructional leadership program for principals, and another district had teachers directly involved in building an effective professional development program.

195. Caldwell, S.D. (1989). *Staff development: A handbook of effective practices.* Oxford, OH: National Staff Development Council.

A practical, concise overview of effective staff development practices. Each chapter includes a list of the knowledge, skills, and attitudes staff developers need to implement successful programs. Most chapters contain an annotated bibliography for readers who want to study a strategy more completely. This volume addresses five major topics: the context in which staff development occurs, the processes of effective staff development, the content addressed in staff development efforts, the foundations of staff development, and the competencies needed by staff developers.

196. Dusewicz, R.A., & Beyer, F.S. (1988). *Dimensions of excellence scales: Survey instruments for school improvement.* (ERIC Document Reproduction Service No. ED 302 590).

Describes the Dimensions of Excellence Scales (DOES) and their use. The DOES have been developed to assist local education agencies in their efforts to diagnose problems, identify strengths, and improve school operations. There are survey scales for school staff, parents, and students. Each scale concerns dimensions that have been found related to effective school performance and that are subject to modification. Dimensions include: school climate, leadership, teacher behavior, curriculum, monitoring and assessment, student discipline and behavior, staff development, and parent involvement.

197. Duttweiler, P.C., & Hord, S.M. (1987). Resources for administrator assessment and staff development. (ERIC Document Reproduction Service No. ED 334 629)

This report synthesizes the literature on administrator assessment and staff development and provides a directory of resources. The components of effective staff development systems, including guidelines and a checklist for planning and implementation are also presented. Finally, descriptions of 27 national programs and resources are included.

198. Guskey, T.R. (1985). Staff development and teacher change. *Educational Leadership, 42* (7), 57–60.

Identifies how teacher change may be accomplished through an effective staff development program. The three major outcomes of effective staff development programs are changes in teachers' beliefs and attitudes, teachers' instructional practices, and students' learning outcomes. Change may be initiated through staff development and provides opportunities to create other initiatives for change in the educational process.

Jacobson, S.L., & Conway, J.A. Cited above as item 53.

199. Joyce, B., & Showers, B. (1988). *Student achievement through staff development.* New York: Longman.

Focuses on student learning as the center of education. While staff development will benefit its personnel, the professional function of the educators' growth is the growth of children. This book presses toward a future in which the investment in teachers and administrators will be adequate and time for study will be part of their work.

200. Kelley, L.S. (1990). Using 4MAT to improve staff development, curriculum assessment, and planning. *Educational Leadership, 48* (2), 38–39.

Describes how schools may use the 4MAT concept to structure the staff development efforts to manage the integration of innovations in curriculum and instruction. Staff development may be a tool to help educators to come to a fundamental understanding of the connection between curriculum and learning.

201. Killion, J.P., et al. (1989). People developer: A new role for principals. *Journal of Staff Development, 10* (1), 2–7.

This article identifies knowledge principals need to guide staff development. The establishment of district staff development programs and intervention for principals having problems utilizing staff development are two recommendations.

202. Levine, M. (1991). Creating effective schools: Findings and implications from research and practice. *Phi Delta Kappan, 72* (4), 389–393.

Provides a variety of approaches for improving staff development. The use of stipends for in-service training, extension of the work year to allow planning and organizational time, and the reduction of teachers' duty periods are some of the concepts discussed. School-based management offers a way to promote consensus and the establishing of these staff development improvement programs.

203. McGreal, T.L. (1989). Necessary ingredients for successful instructional improvement initiatives. *Journal of Staff Development, 10* (1), 35–41.

Presents five key ingredients for successful instructional improvement initiatives in district-wide programs: (1) leadership density, (2) knowledge of the literature, (3) sense of priorities and realistic perspective on available energies and resources, (4) development of a framework for teaching, and (5) a teacher evaluation system complementary to the improvement of instruction.

204. Neubert, G.A., & Bratton, E.C. (1987). Team coaching: Staff development side by side. *Educational Leadership, 44* (5), 29–32.

Describes how peer coaching may provide for effective staff development when visiting resource teachers teach alongside their counterparts. Success is demonstrated by the peer coach not as an observer but as a participating teacher. The knowledge transfer allows for new teachers to learn and receive support and facilitation during the coaching activity.

205. Nevi, C. (1986). Half-truths that hinder staff development. *Principal, 65* (3), 44–46.

Outlines six beliefs administrators may have that hinder the deliverance of good staff development programs. The author asserts that it is important that principals critically examine the implications of these beliefs.

206. Peters, D.L. (1988). Current issues and future needs in staffing training. (ERIC Document Reproduction Service No. ED 305 139).

Research and experience suggest that a systematic plan of personnel development should be implemented. This plan should include five tiers of activity: (1) in-service training and orientation for entry level personnel; (2) training and education during service for teachers and caregivers concerned with improving their teaching skills; (3) professional education and credentialing in four- or five-year programs; (4) specialist preparation for professionals ready to assume leadership roles; and

(5) senior leadership preparation for leaders of the profession. The author also discusses ways in which the tier system might be used to increase the number of qualified personnel, particularly minority group members.

207. Purcell, L.O. (1987). Principal's role in staff development. (ERIC Document Reproduction Service No. ED 285 279).

Research indicates that one critical factor in successful and continuous staff development is consistently strong leadership and support. Drawing on recent studies, this paper summarizes the importance of the principal's support for staff development as an agent for school level change. Principals who understand and participate in staff development activities gain credibility and visibility with staff and parents alike.

208. Showers, B., Joyce, B., & Bennett, B. (1987). Synthesis of research on staff development: A framework for future study and a state-of-the-art analysis. *Educational Leadership, 45* (3), 82–87.

Details a synthesis of research on staff development identifying the key components of effective programs. The meta-analysis of the research studies provides numerous highlights for principals to use in developing and implementing staff development programs.

209. Smith, W.F., & Andrews, R.L. (1989). *Instructional leadership: How principals make a difference.* Alexandria, VA: Association for Supervision and Curriculum Development.

Relates how the principal makes the difference as an instructional leader by performing the role of providing evaluation and staff development concepts for faculty. The principal is expected to be a resource provider to meet the developmental needs of the faculty.

210. Stephens, E.C. (1990). Make staff development the heart of school improvement. *Executive Educator, 12* (11), 24–25.

The principal's true role in promoting positive change through staff development. Includes commitment, collaboration, communication, and coordination.

211. Urso, I. (1990). Teacher development through global education. In. K. A. Tye *Global education: From thought to action.* Alexandria, VA: Association for Supervision and Curriculum Development, 100–109.

Describes how global education can be an encouraging force for teacher development. With the changes occurring in the world, teachers should become aware of the impact these changes will have on their students. Staff development programs should address the global education needs for educators.

212. Wildman, T.M., & Niles, J.A. (1987). Essentials of professional growth. *Educational Leadership, 44* (5), 4–10.

Describes how collaboration and interaction between novice teachers and experienced teachers can assist in their own learning. Teachers should be involved in determining the conditions for professional growth and have input in the programs for training. The authors discuss the profiles of professional development styles and the characteristics for personal growth.

CHAPTER 15
Measurement and Evaluation

With new demands on education and educational programs, assessment systems are constantly being challenged. The driving force behind these challenges is an attempt to build a new assessment system based on the vague goals and standards established for schools. Two of the national goals for the year 2000 address student achievement directly; challenging subject matter and the replacement of students in first place in mathematics and science achievement.

BACKGROUND

The National Commission on the Principalship (Thomson, 1990) identified key skills the principal should develop to successfully measure student achievement: (1) determining what diagnostic information is needed about students, staff, and the school environment; (2) examining the extent to which outcomes meet or exceed previously defined standards, goals, or priorities for individuals or groups; (3) drawing inferences for program revisions; (4) interpreting measurements or evaluations for others; (5) relating programs to desired outcomes; and (6) developing equivalent measures of competence (p. 23–24).

WHO DECIDES?

The principal must be aware of efforts to develop a national student assessment system as well as local school assessment systems. There are many questions concerning the multitude of assessment proposals. The principal must use a school team to determine which of these are congruent with the views of the school (Hanson, 1991). Individuals at the school level must be involved in (1) determining the diagnostic environment; (2) examining the outcomes to be met; and (3) determining the standards for assessment. From these data, program revisions may be developed to enhance the educational program. Gronlund and Linn (1990) indicate that the principal should use teacher knowledge and effective information processing and decision-making styles to develop assessment standards.

ASSESSMENT AND CURRICULUM CONGRUENCE

Measurement and evaluation are essential for education, but should not be detrimental to the curriculum. Assessment systems must be related to the values and philosophy of the school/district and be directly related to the curriculum. Curriculum changes must be related to the performance of students based on the assessment system. As a national assessment system is developed, schools must develop school level assessment systems congruent with the national system. The key for developing the local assessment system is to identify (1) the needs of students, (2) the outcomes expected, and (3) methods of determining if students have mastered these desired outcomes (Ebel & Frisbie, 1991). Principals are expected to use evaluation processes to determine the effectiveness of the school regarding student achievement. The school assessment system should be varied and provide different options to be evaluated. The variables for assessment should include needs, plans, operations, and results. The assessment should focus on how well students' needs are being met, while searching for unexpected outcomes, both positive and negative (Payne, 1992).

NOTES

Ebel, R.L., & Frisbie, D.A. (1991). *Essentials of educational measurement*. (5th Ed.). Englewood Cliffs, NJ: Prentice-Hall.

Gronlund, N.E., & Linn, R.L. (1990). *Measurement and evaluation in teaching*. New York: Macmillan.

Hanson, E.M. (1991). *Educational administration and organizational behavior*. Boston: Allyn and Bacon.

Payne, D.A. *Measuring and evaluating educational outcomes*. New York: Merrill.

Thomson, S.D. (1990). *Principals for our changing schools: Preparation and certification*. Fairfax, VA: National Commission on the Principalship.

BIBLIOGRAPHY

213. Archbald, D.A., & Newmann, F.M. (1988). *Beyond standardized testing: Assessing authentic academic achievement in the secondary school.* Reston, VA: National Association of Secondary School Principals.

This book, designed as an assessment of standardized testing, is a framework for thinking systemically about assessment. A review of the uses and limitations of standardized tests and descriptions of several methods that may offer more helpful approaches to assessment are provided.

214. Brandt, R.S. (1989). On misuse of testing: A conversation with George Madaus. *Educational Leadership, 46* (7), 26–29.

An interview with George Madaus explaining how the misuse of test data corrupts the inferences drawn from them. Madaus calls for cost-benefit evaluations and challenges educators to seek better accountability methods, test student samples, use multiple indicators, and include teacher judgment in the process.

215. Crooks, T.J. (1988). The impact of classroom evaluation practices on students. *Review of Educational Research, 58* (4), 438–481.

Identifies the way results are summarized from fourteen fields of research that clarify the relationships between classroom evaluation and student outcomes. Conclusions are merged to produce an integrated summary with clear implications for effective education. Classroom evaluation has direct/indirect and positive/negative impacts on student performance.

216. Duran, R.P. (1989). Assessment and instruction of at-risk Hispanic students. *Exceptional Children, 56* (2), 154–158.

The author states the limitations on standardized test use with Hispanic students. Recent research developments support the use of testing and assessment as tools for promoting learning. Assisted performance and dynamic assessment are discussed in the context of individual education plans and a cycle for test-train-test principles.

217. Engle, P. (1991). Tracking progress toward the school readiness goal. *Educational Leadership, 48* (5), 39–42.

Explains systems currently being developed that will enable schools to assess the readiness of young children based on knowledge about child development. With new national goals on education for preschool children, these systems provide an opportunity for a principal to identify the readiness concepts which may apply to children of the school.

218. Gray, P.A. (1990). *Assessment of basic oral communication skills. A selected, annotated bibliography.* (2nd ed.). Annandale, VA: Speech Communication Association.

This book contains 44 references, dated 1976 to 1989, that do the following: (1) outline broad assessment issues; (2) review a variety of test instruments; (3) report assessment practices throughout the states; and (4) focus specifically on the assessment of speaking, listening, and functional communication skills.

219. Haertel, E., & Calfee, R. (1983). School achievement: Thinking about what to test. *Journal of Educational Measurement, 20* (2), 119–32.

The history of the relationship between achievement tests and curriculum programs is reviewed, and it is concluded that content specialists are best qualified as sources of curriculum goals to specify content, kinds of attainment, and standards.

220. Heibert, E.H., & Calfee, R.C. (1989). Advancing academic literacy through teachers' assessments. *Educational Leadership, 47* (7), 50–54.

Discusses the use of student portfolios and other assessment records as compared to the individual teacher assessments. The system described limits use of teacher-gathered assessments by other interested parties. For school-related decisions, standardized test scores are recommended for use in conjunction with teachers' assessments.

221. Kubiszyn, T., & Borich, G. (1990). *Educational testing and measurement.* Glenview, IL: Scott, Foresman.

Provides an overview for developing effective tests and the use of test and measurement systems for student assessment. The aspects of testing related to the instructional goals and objectives in measuring learning outcomes are addressed. The elements of administering, analyzing, and improving the test based on research are presented.

222. Martinez, M.E., & Lipson, J.I. (1989). Assessment for learning. *Educational Leadership, 46* (7), 73–75.

Describes the essential elements of new test innovations and shows how they might promote learning. The facets needed to create the tests are indicated. The concepts of mastery systems envisioned by the Educational Testing Service will: (1) provide immediate, elaborate feedback; (2) identify learning progress through mapping; and (3) present real-life test questions.

223. Mills, R.P. (1989). Portfolios capture rich array of student performance. *School Administrator, 46* (11), 8–11.

Vermont educators, with citizen support, have decided to use portfolios of student work. Standardized tests will play an important, although secondary, role. Student and teacher responsibility will increase dramatically.

224. Mitchell, J.V., Jr., Wise, S.L., & Plake, B.S. (1990). *Assessment of teaching: Purposes, practices, and implications for the profession.* Hillsdale, NJ: Lawrence Erlbaum Associates.

Relates the importance of teaching assessment and the impact of American education on world society. The authors examine teacher assessment in terms of its sociological, psychological, legal, political, contextual, psychometric, and practical applications. Current assessment methods are discussed and directions toward future methods of teacher assessment are identified.

225. Nickerson, R.S. (1989). New directions in educational assessment. *Educational Researcher, 18* (9), 3–7.

Discusses the issues involved in the construction, validity, and use of tests that evaluate educational progress of students. Emphasis is on assessing the higher-order cognitive functioning skills.

226. Olson, J.B. (1990). Development, implementation, and validation of a computerized test for statewide assessment. *Educational Measurement: Issues and Practice, 9* (2), 7–10, 32.

WICAT skills assessment test, a computerized testing system for state assessment objectives, is described. Results in Texas support the feasibility of district-wide computerized testing.

227. Paulson, F.L., Paulson, P.R., & Meyer, C.A. (1991). What makes a portfolio a portfolio? *Educational Leadership, 48* (5), 60–63.

Provides insight into one district's use of portfolios for student assessment. Many questions are generated from the consideration of how portfolios may be used, what they should contain, and the inferences which might be drawn from them.

228. Phillips, G.W., & Finn, C.E., Jr. (1990). State-by-state comparisons can benefit education. *Educational Leadership, 47* (7), 43–55.

The authors propose that state-by-state comparisons will benefit education. This is based on the 1992 plans for the National Assessment of Educational Progress to assess math skills at fourth- and eighth-grade levels and reading skills among fourth graders. This will be the first time that a process has been developed and implemented to compare states.

229. Radocy, R.E. (1989). Evaluating student achievement. *Music Educators Journal, 76* (4), 30–33.

The author identifies the underlying concepts of student evaluation and offers suggestions for evaluating musical achievement. The article maintains that all evaluations are subjective, and suggests techniques for minimizing the subjectivity.

230. Rosenfeld, S., & Shinn, M.R. (Eds.). (1989). Mini-series on curriculum-based assessment. *School Psychology Review, 18* (3), 297–370.

Five articles and a commentary on curriculum-based assessment (CBA) are presented. Article topics include a comparison of CBA models, computer applications, development of written retell for CBA in secondary programs, development of math skills in low-achieving high school students via CBA, and methods of summarizing trends in student achievement.

231. Rudner, L.M., Conoley, J.C., & Plake, B.S. (1989). *Understanding achievement tests: A guide for school administrators.* Washington, DC: American Institutes for Research and ERIC Clearinghouse on Tests, Measurement and Evaluation. (ED 314 426)

This guide opens with a discussion of the basic principles of testing. Current information is provided for school district staff about selecting and administering tests. Addresses of major test publishers, and a glossary of testing terms are also included.

232. Shepard, L.A. (1989). Why we need better assessments. *Educational Leadership, 46* (7), 4–9.

Indicates that in today's political climate, standardized tests are inadequate and misleading as achievement measures. The author proposes that educators should employ a variety of measures, improve standardized test content and format, and remove incentives for teaching to the test. As the focus is on raising test scores, the validity of the tests are distorted.

233. Stiggins, R.J. (1989). Measuring thinking skills through classroom assessment. *Journal of Educational Measurement, 26* (3), 233–46.
Identifies assessment procedures used by classroom teachers to determine the extent to which the teachers measured students' higher order thinking skills in mathematics, science, social studies, and language arts. The research provides insight into assessment concepts as applied regarding student performance.

234. Stiggins, R.J. (1988). Revitalizing classroom assessment: The highest instructional priority. *Phi Delta Kappan, 69* (5), 363–68.
Teachers may spend as much as 40 percent of their time directly involved in assessment-related activities, yet most teachers are not trained or prepared for this demanding task.

235. Wiggins, G. (1991). Standards, not standardization: Evoking quality student work. *Educational Leadership, 48* (5), 18–25.
In this article, the author insists that standards for students and quality work are to be established at the local level. It is at the school where the standards must be internalized and upheld by every teacher in the classroom. Students at all levels should be expected to do high quality work evaluated against a single standard of excellence.

236. Wiggins, G. (1989). Teaching to the (authentic) test. *Educational Leadership, 46* (7), 41–47.
Stresses that instead of being devices for measuring what students have learned, tests should be instructional. These concepts become the vehicle for clarifying and setting intellectual standards. To regain control over assessment, schools need to rethink their requirements and grading systems.

237. Wiggins, G. (1989). A true test: Toward more authentic and equitable assessment. *Phi Delta Kappan, 70* (9), 703–13.
Educators' confusion over uses of a standardized test is akin to mistaking pulse rate for the total effect of a health examination. Using authentic standards and tests to judge intellectual ability is labor-intensive and time consuming.

238. Wolf, D.P. (1989). Portfolio assessment: Sampling student work. *Educational Leadership, 46* (7), 35–39.

Points out how alternatives to standardized assessment were determined by a group of researchers through use of the portfolio. The researchers identify the value of portfolios in student assessment.

CHAPTER 16

Resource Allocation

Resource allocation involves many tasks as identified by the National Commission for the Principalship (Thomson, 1990): (1) planning and developing the budget with appropriate staff; (2) seeking, allocating, and adjusting fiscal, human, and material resources; (3) utilizing the physical plant; (4) monitoring resource use; and (5) reporting results. Prasch (1990) suggests that the role of the principal in school-based management [SBM] will require similar skills. One of the major aspects of SBM is resource allocation controlled by planning (Elmore, 1988). The budget process must be developed in an interactive arrangement with appropriate staff and committees.

PLANNING

The planning concepts identified by the National Commission for the Principalship apply to the allocation of fiscal, human and material resources as needed by the school (Kimbrough & Burkett, 1990). The utilization of the school facility also requires extensive planning by the principal and supporting committees. Garrett, Flanigan, and Richardson (1991) suggest that evaluation for effective principals should include emphasis on principals' performance in the areas of resource management, school budget, and school plant operations.

FINANCE

With the magnitude of the public school finance system, a school principal should be knowledgeable about sources of income and principles governing expenditures. State and local district policies may control the principal's freedom to determine the budget and allocation of resources within the school operation (Knezevich, 1984). Principals should understand research on resource allocation as related to (1) instruction, (2) effectiveness of instruction, (3) student achievement, and (4) cost-effectiveness. The multitude of resources must be considered and shared with others in the decision making and planning processes. Educational reform demands additional accountability, and the principal must be prepared to allocate resources according to need and availability.

SCHOOL PLANT

School plant management is more than assigning classrooms, it also includes planning effective utilization to carry out the school curriculum. Principals should also implement strategic planning or synergetic planning to organize site usage. Facility maintenance must also be addressed when the principal assigns custodial staff. The principal must plan for repairs to the school building in order to minimize disruptions to the educational processes.

REPORTING

The principal is responsible for monitoring the resources used and reporting the results to supraordinates and subordinates (Hoy & Miskel, 1991). The monitoring process involves inventory control and expenditure control including how resources have been spent to benefit the educational process. The emphasis of school reform is on student achievement and cost-effectiveness. The principal is responsible to assure the public that funds have been allocated and expended appropriately.

SUMMARY

The principal must develop skills to meet the changing demands for effective schools and manage limited resources for maximum utilization. With the education reform movement this is even a greater factor in the success of the principal as an educational leader.

NOTES

Elmore, R.F. (1988). *Early experiences in restructuring schools: Voices from the field.* Washington, DC: National Governor's Association.

Garrett, W.R., Flanigan, J.L., & Richardson, M.D. (1991, March). Removing the barriers to effectiveness: A theoretical and practical approach to principal evaluation. A paper presented at the annual meeting of the American Association of School Administrators, New Orleans, LA.

Hoy, W.K., & Miskel, C.G. (1991). *Educational administration: Theory, research, and practice.* New York: McGraw-Hill.

Kimbrough, R.B., & Burkett, C.W. (1990). *The principalship: Concepts and practices.* Englewood Cliffs, NJ: Prentice-Hall.

Knezevich, S.J. (1984). *Administration of public education.* (4th Ed.). New York: Harper & Row.

BIBLIOGRAPHY

239. Agron, J. (1990). Special program produces surprising results on education attitudes. *American School & University, 63* (2), 20.

Describes the impact special television programs have had on public support for education. Emphasizes that taxpayers would be willing to pay more if the money went to the neighborhood school. Education was identified as one of the top three problems facing the country today.

Ashbaugh, C.R., & Kasten, K.L. Cited above as item 49.

240. Basham, V., & Lunenburg, F.C. (1989). Strategic planning, student achievement and school district financial and demographic factors. *Planning & Change, 20* (3), 158–171.

Describes research concerning strategic planning and the impact on student achievement of a school district's financial and demographic factors. Emphasizes the need to spend education dollars on students to have an impact on student achievement.

241. Black, S. (1991). Cut without killing. *The American School Board Journal, 178* (5), 31–33.

Deals with how to cut a budget using a zero-based curriculum model. When making budget cuts reason, rather than emotion, must be used. Five rules for budget cutters are presented, and seven tiers for making adjustments in the budget that ease the pain of making cuts are listed. This is a no-nonsense way of making budget cuts.

242. Burrup, P.E., & Brimley, V., Jr. (1989). *Financing education in a climate of change.* Boston: Allyn and Bacon, Inc.

Provides an extensive review of the economics of education, sources of local revenue, and finance systems for use in education. With education reform being a major issue, the authors indicate the concepts and principles affecting the financial equity of education.

243. Castaldi, B. (1987). *Educational facilities: Planning, modernization, and management.* Boston: Allyn and Bacon.

Theory is related to application demonstrating how the school administrator must cope with school facilities. The principal's role in maintenance and operation are discussed. The school principal has responsibility for the facility.

244. Council of Educational Facility Planners, International. (1990). *Computer facilities planning: A guide for school districts, architects and contractors.* (1990). Columbus, OH: CEFPI.

Based on research from Apple Computer, Inc., this book provides planning concepts school administrators should apply in developing facilities for computer technology. The guide addresses the role of the project manager, new facility planning, existing facility planning, special problems and issues, and network capabilities.

245. Educational Facility Planners, International. *School planning and design.* (1990). Columbus, OH: CEFPI.

Provides school administrators information on contemporary issues that affect the planning and design of educational facilities for the 1990s. The goals of the guide are to examine the critical elements of school planning and design, to explore the current trends in school planning and design, to discuss how quality planning and design can enhance the educational process, and to discuss how to best address tomorrow's technology in today's school facilities.

246. Fitter, F. (1991). Look at the school that grants built. *The American School Board Journal, 178* (5), 34–35.

A report on Holyoke, Massachusetts, schools that created a new magnet middle school with grant funding. Fund raising tips are presented, and the report presents a way for schools that are strapped financially to get the extra money needed to run innovative programs.

247. Graves, B.E. (1990). Addressing future concerns of administrators. *American School & University, 63* (1), 16.

Describes the need for the educational facilities planner of the future to address such topics as: (1) the rapidly changing demography, (2) shift of teachers, (3) financial planning, (4) security, (5) technology, and (6) bond issues. The author emphasizes the impact technology will have on the future of facility planning.

248. Gutherie, F., Garms, W., & Pierce, L. (1988). *School finance and education policy: Enhancing educational efficiency, equality, and choice.* Englewood Cliffs, NJ: Prentice Hall.

Identifies the many changes occurring in education with regard to school finance and education policy. Concepts which have made an impact on educational funding for efficiency and equality are discussed. With education reform and limited funds for education, creative financing and the use of priorities are essential.

249. Hamm, R.W., & Crosser, S. (1991). School fees. *The American School Board Journal, 178* (6), 29–31.

Presents a breakdown of the use of fees by schools, state-by-state, in chart form. A case for no fees is made by the authors who believe in the ideal of a free public education.

250. Hartley, H.J. (1989). Budgeting for the 1990s. *The School Administrator, 46* (4), 31, 34, 36.

A list of prerequisites to successful budgeting is stated and a checklist for evaluating local school budgets is presented. A short article on how to make and evaluate a budget.

251. Kowalski, T. (1989). *Planning and managing school facilities.* Westport, CT: Greenwood Press.

Provides the school administrator the basic components for planning and managing school facilities. Planning a facility and applying specifications for educational purposes are related to the management components of maintaining the facility.

252. McKenzie, J.A. (1991). How to survive the funding drought. *The American School Board Journal, 178* (3), 23–25.

The author is the former superintendent of the Tredyffrin/ Easttown School District in Berwyn, Pennsylvania. The article is an explanation of how a tax hike was promoted and passed by using software as a means of explaining the need for the tax hike.

253. Moore, D.P. (Ed.). (1991). *Guide for planning educational facilities.* Columbus, OH: The Council of Educational Facility Planners, International.

Provides an insight into the historical development of educational facilities. Emphasizes the planning stages school administrators should use in developing new educational facilities or renovating old facilities. Educational specifications are identified for developing effective school buildings as related to the goals and objectives of the school district and the curriculum.

254. Natale, J.A. (1991). Get savvy about budgeting. *The American School Board Journal, 178* (3), 19–22, 38.

Presents information for school board members on how to cut budgets and gain public support for the cuts.

255. Orenstein, A.C. (1989). Trimming the fat, stretching the meat for 1990s budgets. *The School Administrator, 46* (9), 20–21.
An overview of what may happen in 1990s' school budgeting.

256. Quest, J. (1990). Prepare your facilities for future technology. *American School & University, 63* (2), 32–33.
Describes how retrofitting space now can benefit upcoming programs concerning technology. Planning anticipated educational facilities may generate new financial demands on a school district. Design and planning for networking concepts is a challenge and should provide for flexibility for changes as new technology is developed.

257. Sanders, K.P., & Thiemann, F.C. (1990). Student costing: An essential tool in site based budgeting and teacher empowerment. *NASSP Bulletin, 74* (523), 95–102.
Stresses that teachers must commit themselves to working on the budget and be actively involved in the budget decision making. School-based budgeting is a major method of empowering teachers and administrators. The article presents ways to determine the cost for a student in a course for the school-year. This is a resource for school-based management.

258. Schaeffer, D., & Shifflette, J. (1990). Transportation for community-based education. *American School & University, 63* (2), 26–27.
Identifies the concepts involved in an effective transportation system for community and schools in a county school district. Scheduling, equipment and drivers, management operations, and proactive planning of transportation issues for the future are discussed.

259. Trotter, A. (1990). Buying trouble. *American School Board Journal, 177* (11), 16–18.
Purchasing practices can get out of hand—especially in the high-stakes educational technology market. Teachers and principals are under siege by vendors to purchase computer equipment. A recommendation is to develop a vendor-customer relations plan.

260. Verstegen, D.A. (1990). Education fiscal policy in the Reagan administration. *Educational Evaluation and Policy Analysis, 12* (4), 355–373.
Discusses the impact of federal spending on decentralizing domestic education programs. Federal government shifts in education spending are

discussed. Education policy and finance changes at the national level are presented.

SECTION FOUR
INTERPERSONAL SKILLS

CHAPTER 17

Motivation

The study of human motivation is difficult and important—difficult because of the subject matter, lack of empirical data, problems of human subjects involved, lack of consensus of a philosophical base; important because of its value and utility of application. Learning theorists dismiss explanations of instinct, psychic forces, as well as reasons why people do what they do, stating instead that all human response is learned.

BACKGROUND

Considerable evidence—declining SAT scores, unfavorable international comparisons of students' performance, documentation that the best college students shun teaching while the best teachers abandon the profession altogether—suggest that the problems with schools are more substantive than superficial (Johnson, 1986). Is there anyone left in schools who is willing to teach? Has all this bad press removed people from the classroom who were capable of teaching? If there are good teachers left, is there any motivation left in those persons to teach? How do principals build the morale and motivation back into their teachers? How do they motivate teachers to go out and do a good job? How do they get teachers to give 110 percent, with just a 2 percent pay raise? How do principals get and maintain educational excellence in their schools?

All levels of administration should be concerned with the above questions. Without teachers who are motivated to teach, the search for educational excellence will be in vain. Principals should continually explore ways to motivate teachers and staff. While teachers generally agree that they are not paid enough for the job they do, they tend to be more motivated if other conditions of the working environment are improved.

WHY STUDY MOTIVATION?

In his research on motivation, William James (1980) found that the average employee in an organization works at only 20 to 30 percent of his ability. However, when highly motivated, employees will work at 80 to 90 percent of their abilities (Hersey & Blanchard, 1977).

MOTIVATION DEFINITIONS

Motivation has been defined in many ways:

. . . the contemporary (immediate) influence on the direction, vigor, and persistence of action (Atkinson & Raynor, 1974).

. . . a process governing choices made by persons or lower organisms among alternative forms of voluntary activity (Vroom, 1964).

. . . motivation has to do with a set of independent/dependent variable relationships that explain the direction, amplitude, and persistence of an individual's behavior, holding constant the effects of aptitude, skill, and understanding of the task, and the constraints operating in the environment (Campbell & Pritchard, 1976).

. . . an inner state that energizes, activates, or moves, and that directs or channels behavior toward goals (Berelson & Steiner, 1964).

. . . a statement of the conditions under which an organization can induce its members to continue their participation, and hence assure organization survival (March & Simon, 1958).

Motivators are the factors that arouse, direct, and sustain increased performance (Duttweiler, 1986).

THEORIES OF MOTIVATION

There are many theories of motivation which are currently espoused by numerous social scientists.

1. The *Content* or *Substantive* theories are concerned with the specific identity of *what* is within an individual or his environment that energizes and sustains behavior. That is, what specific things motivate people.

    a. Maslow's Needs Theories
    b. Hertzberg's "Satisfiers" and "Dissatisfiers"
    c. McClelland's Achievement Motivation
    d. DeCharm's Personal Causation Theory

2. *The Process or Mechanical Theories* are concerned about *how* behavior is energized, directed, sustained and stopped. They generally describe the major classes of factors that are important and how the factors interact and influence one another.
    a. Vroom's Expectancy Theory
    b. Adams' Equity Theory
    c. Deci's Cognitive Evaluation Theory
    d. Stimulus Response or Drive vs. Habit Theories

Hertzberg's (1966) two-factor theory, or the motivator-hygiene theory emerged from his now famous study of industrial employees' motivation to work.

1. Motivators— (also called intrinsic factors, the satisfiers and job content factors)

    when gratified, they increase job satisfaction

    when not gratified, they do not increase job satisfaction

2. Hygienes—(also called the maintenance factor, the extrinsic factor, the dissatisfiers and the job context factor)

    when not gratified, negative attitudes are created causing dissatisfaction

    when gratified, they do not cause satisfaction

SERGIOVANNI AND HERZBERG IN EDUCATION

Thomas Sergiovanni (1966) replicated Hertzberg's work in educational organizations. His findings supported the assertion that satisfiers (motivators) and dissatisfiers (hygienes) tend to be mutually exclusive. There were some differences:

1. The work itself and advancement were not significant motivators (teaching is considered a terminal position; there are several

     aspects of the work, attendance, scheduling, hall duty, etc.) that lead to dissatisfaction.

2. Teachers tend to also differ from business employees in having more problems with subordinates (students) than with superordinates.

Sergiovanni's (1966) work has led him to identify some teachers who apparently are hygiene or extrinsic reward seekers. His study revealed that two-thirds of the respondents were motivation-seekers, one-fourth were hygiene seekers, and the remaining 8 percent fell in between.

Sergiovanni (1966) classified the hygiene seekers into three groups:

1. Those who have the potential for motivation seeking but are frustrated by insensitive and closed administrative, supervisory, and organization policies and practices.
2. Those who have the potential for motivation seeking but who elect to channel this potential into other (non-professional or non-school) areas of their lives.
3. Those who do not have the potential for motivation seeking on or off the job.

The motivation seekers fit into the group of educators whose primary needs are higher level ones and who are most responsive to intrinsic rewards.

Sergiovanni's (1966) studies showed that achievement, recognition, and responsibility contributed the most satisfaction teachers felt from their work. Other studies show that teacher job satisfaction is likely when what a teacher perceives as getting through a job matches what he/she perceives as needing from the job (Kreis & Milstein, 1985).

ADMINISTRATOR'S USE OF MOTIVATION

Administrators typically use one of five approaches to motivate people. They are:

a)	be strong	Theory X, Taylor's Scientific Management
b)	be good	provide dissatisfiers of Herzberg
c)	implicit bargaining	learned stimulus-responses
d)	competition	misapplication of TA
e)	internalized motivation	higher level need of Maslow, job satisfiers of Herzberg

To maximize productivity in school settings, the administrator must take the position that people, if given opportunities to achieve and meet personal needs, will work most productively in a situation where self-expression and direction is valued. Structured work assignments, accordingly, rely on the internalized motivation of the "professional" employee.

MOTIVATION AND MERIT PAY

Most states that have tried to improve education have done so with some type of incentive pay for teachers (Doyle & Hartle, 1985). The idea is that if teachers are paid better they will teach better. Merit pay and career ladders have been the solution most states have chosen to motivate teachers to do a better job of teaching. In the profit-making world, merit pay has limited application; it works only where there is a clear "bottom line." Among nonprofit and public sector organizations, such criteria rarely exist (Csikszentmihaly & McCormack, 1986).

Merit pay for teaching the same subject better than the teacher in the next classroom poses formidable problems (Doyle & Hartle, 1985). Teachers should not be made to compete with each other regarding who can teach a particular subject the best. This form of merit pay often results in bitter feelings and low morale. Teachers should be rewarded for a job well done both by recognition programs and by pay that tells the teachers they are worthy of the profession they have chosen (Blase, Strathe, & Pajak, 1986).

MOTIVATION AND TEACHER INVOLVEMENT

Teachers should have a major input into the schooling process. Teachers tend to be more satisfied with their job if they feel that they are a major component in the decision-making process. Teachers should be given opportunities to work together to solve problems in their school. Allowing teachers the opportunity to interact with each other gives them a feeling that they are not in the job alone. It allows for comparison of teaching strategies and for the release of frustrations that a teacher may be experiencing. Japanese management or Theory Z when applied to schools also impacts teacher motivation through shared governance, shared decision making, motivation through high self-interest, and long-term rewards (Ouchi, 1982). In isolated settings, teachers believe they alone are responsible for running their classrooms and that to do so successfully requires a maximum amount of autonomy (Rosenholtz, 1985).

TEACHER STRESS

Other factors that need to be considered in teacher motivation include teacher stress. Many teachers have complained about the amount of paperwork that is required of them. Paperwork often calls for much of the teachers time which puts stress on the teacher and students when it comes to actual classroom teaching (Goldman, 1985). Teachers experience stress and job dissatisfaction in the following areas: disruptive and violent students, fear of violence, lack of public and parent support and respect, lack of job security, lack of job mobility, lack of other career options, poor working conditions, inadequate salary and benefits, excessive paperwork, poor relationships with others in the work setting, lack of personal recognition, and loss of control over what happens within one's classroom (Wangberg, 1984).

Principals need to look at all these areas and try to buffer the teacher from as many of these disruptions as possible. If these are not removed teachers may become demotivated. Bjorkquist (1982) listed six phases of demotivation that will affect teachers: 1) confusion, 2) anger, 3) subconscious hope, 4) disillusionment, 5) uncooperativeness, and 6) departure.

SUMMARY

Motivated teachers will work harder, feel better about themselves and the job they are doing, and provide students with greater opportunities for a better education (McLaughlin, Pfeifer, Swanson-Owens, & Yee, 1986).

NOTES

Atkinson, J.W., & Raynor, J.O. (1974). *Motivation and achievement.* New York: Halsted.

Berelson, B., & Steiner, G.A. (1964). *Human behavior: An inventory of scientific findings.* New York: Harcourt, Brace, and World.

Bjorkquist, D.C. (1982). *Supervision in vocational education: Management of human resources,* pp. 125-126. Boston: Allyn and Bacon.

Blase, J.J., Strathe, M.I., & Pajak, E.F. (1986). A theory of teacher performance: Preservice and inservice implications. *Contemporary Education, 57* (4), 138-143.

Campbell, J.P., & Pritchard, R.D. (1976). Motivation theory in industrial and organization theory. In M.D. Dunnette (ed.) *Handbook of industrial and organizational psychology.* Chicago: Rand-McNally.

Csikszentmihalyi, M., & McCormack, J. (1986). The influence of teachers. *Phi Delta Kappan, 67* (6), 415-419.

Doyle, D.P., & Hartle, W. (1985). Leadership in education: Governors, legislators, and teachers. *Phi Delta Kappan, 67,* (1), 21-27.

Duttweiler, P.C. (1986). Educational excellence and motivating teachers. *Clearing House, 59* (8), 371-374.

Goldman, J.J. (1985). Schools "r" us. *Clearing House, 59* (2), 72-74.

Hersey, P., & Blanchard, K.H. (1977). *Management of organizational behavior.* Englewood Cliffs, NJ: Prentice-Hall.

Herzberg, F.W. (1966). *Work and the nature of man.* Cleveland, OH: World.

James, W. (1980). *Principles of psychology.* New York: Holt, Rinehart, and Winston.

Johnson, S.M. (1986). Incentives for teachers: What motivates, what matters. *Educational Administration Quarterly, 22* (3), 54-79.

Kreis, K., & Milstein, M. (1985). Satisfying teacher's needs. *Clearing House, 59* (2), 75-77.

March, J.G., & Simon, H.A. (1958). *Organizations.* New York: Wiley.

McLaughlin, M.W., Pfeifer, R.S., Swanson-Owens, D., & Yee, S. (1986). Why teachers won't teach. *Phi Delta Kappan, 67* (6), 420-426.

Ouchi, W.G. (1982). Theory Z and the schools. *School Administration, 39* (4), 12-19.

Rosenholtz, S.J. (1985). Effective schools: Interpreting the evidence. *American Journal of Education, 93* (3), 352-388.

Sergiovanni, T.J. (1966). Factors which affect satisfaction and dissatisfaction of teachers. *Journal of Educational Administration, 5* (1), 66-82.

Vroom, V.H. (1964). *Work and motivation.* New York: Wiley.

Wangberg, E.G. (1984). The complex issue of teacher stress and job dissatisfaction. *Contemporary Education, 56* (1), 11-15.

BIBLIOGRAPHY

261. Adams, B., & Bailey, G.D. (1989). School is for teachers: Enhancing the school environment. *NASSP Bulletin, 73* (513), 44-48.

Teachers who feel good about themselves and their abilities are the ones most likely to experience success. A personal approach is suggested for principals to use in building teachers' self-esteem through recurring compliments, imagery, social reinforcers, and trust.

262. Ashton, B., & Hollingsworth, J. (1984). Reassignment: Threat or promise? *English Journal, 73* (4), 62-65.

The authors take a humorous and highly personalized view of reassignment within a school system. They develop a model for re-adjustment after being assigned to a new content area. The model is based on four assumptions:

1. Change is a process.
2. It is made first by individuals and then by institutions.
3. It is highly personal.
4. It entails developmental growth in feelings and skills.

The authors suggest that support from the administration and staff in adjusting to the assignment is vital.

263. Barth, T.S. (1984). Must colleagues become adversaries? *Principal, 63* (5), 52-53.

The author states that children's needs cannot be met until a climate of cooperation has been established between the teachers and administrator—that colleagues do not need to become adversaries.

264. Bhella, S. (1982). Principal's leadership style: Does it affect teacher morale? *Education, 102* (4), 369-376.

The author relates research in leadership style and its affect on teacher morale. The author concluded that there was a positive correlation between principals' attitudes toward people and productivity, and there was no relationship between principals' attitudes toward people and teachers' attitudes toward teaching.

265. Blase, J.J. (1984). Teacher coping and school principal behaviors. *Contemporary Education, 56* (1), 21-25.

Blase related his research on teacher stress caused by the behaviors of the principal. The author also looked at the effectiveness of coping strategies used by teachers in dealing with those behaviors. Blase suggests that staff developers and organizational change agents bring teachers and principals together in an effort to find the best way to deal with stress in a collaborative manner.

266. Bredeson, P.V. (1989). *Redefining leadership and the roles of school principals: Responses to changes in the professional worklife of teachers.* (Eric Document Reproduction Service No. ED 304 782).

Bredeson investigates principals' perceptions of the effect of teacher empowerment on their role as building administrators. The researcher conducted structured interviews with 10 principals, five elementary and five secondary, in two school systems. These systems were characterized by their use of shared decision making and greater professional autonomy among teachers and administrators. The author concluded with nine important themes that emerged from these data: (1) the language of shared governance and empowerment; (2) readiness for professional growth and empowerment; (3) the importance of the superintendent's leadership in empowerment; (4) time as a key resource for empowerment; (5) boundary spanning for school principals; (6) enhancement of teachers' and principals' professional image; (7) the importance of hearing teachers' voices; (8) shared professional thinking; and (9) dealing with power through empowerment.

267. Brodinsky, B. (1984). Teacher morale: What builds it, what kills it. *Instructor, 93*(8), 36-38.

Brodinsky reports the findings of a study by the American Association of School Administrators which interviewed 300 teachers and administrators about teacher morale. The article includes problems which both teachers and administrators feel are causes of poor morale. The author lists some morale boosters, such as: shared governance (letting teachers voice their opinions about critical issues and giving them a role in making decisions that affect them); recognition of a job well done; network of support; sense of pride; positive discipline; courtesy and good behavior; communication; internal and external; adequate supplies; materials; and physical setting and inservice.

268. Cameron, D. (1985). An idea that merits consideration. *Phi Delta Kappan, 67* (2), 110-111.

Most merit pay proposals are based on three perilous assumptions. The first is that teachers are not doing a very good job in the classroom and merit pay would give them incentive to improve. The existence of a workable way to reward individual teachers for their performance, that is better than the existing salary schedule, is the second assumption. The third belief is that there are realistic criteria for disbursing merit pay.

269. Chandler, T.A. (1984). Can Theory Z be applied to the public schools? *Education, 104* (4), 343-345.

The author questions the applicability of Theory Z to school districts. Theory Z is a form of management which stresses concern for people. Another tenent of Theory Z is that decisions are made by the people involved coming to a consensus. The theory has been used effectively in Japan. The author appears to support this theory as a means for labor to use in lieu of unions.

270. Davis, J.B. (1984). Indirect means of encouraging change in teachers: A supervisory model or change without coercion. *Contemporary Education, 56* (1), 26-30.

In this article the author suggests indirect ways for a supervisor to encourage teachers to change. Some of these methods are more applicable to situations where the supervisor is also a teacher, but could be modified in some situations where the principal is the supervisor.

The list of suggestions includes:

1. observation of the supervisor,
2. intervisitation,
3. systems of analysis,
4. clinical supervisory approach,
5. analyzing verbal patterns,
6. involve teachers in decision making,
7. analyzing group dynamics.

271. DuFour, R.P. (1986). Must principals choose between teacher morale and effective school? *NASSP Bulletin, 70* (490), 33-37.

Working with an enthusiastic, highly motivated staff and meeting the standards of an "effective school" probably rates at the top of a principal's wish list. Research on employee motivation conducted in the late 1950s and early 1960s noted that salary—along with other extrinsic factors such as working conditions, company policy, and job security—could lead to worker dissatisfaction and to substandard performance. These extrinsic conditions were largely ineffective in motivating employees to extra effort or commitment. Rather, if individuals were to be inspired to exceptional effort, they needed to feel a sense of:

1. the significance of the work they were doing,
2. achievement,
3. recognition for accomplishment, and
4. increased responsibility and advancement.

The key to motivation is "job enrichment," or increasing the autonomy and responsibility of the employee. This enrichment can only occur when administrators are willing to share the decision-making authority. Effective school research indicates that strong instructional leadership from the principal influences student achievement through highly motivated teachers.

272. Ellis, N.H. (1988). *Job redesign: Can it influence teacher motivation?* (Eric Document Reproduction Service No. ED 305-739)

In order to attract people to the teaching profession and to motivate the more capable teachers to remain in the profession, a career structure is needed that will promote excellence, reward commitment, and encourage growth. This study explores the relationships between characteristics of teaching as an occupation and the internal work motivation of teachers. Using a Job Diagnostic Survey based on Hackman's Job Characteristics Model, the study sought data from a random sample of 425 classroom teachers in Fairfield County, Connecticut, to see if these teachers perceived the presence of the core job dimensions of significance, autonomy, and feedback and to ascertain how teachers viewed the motivating potential of their jobs. Also examined were the overall job satisfaction of teachers, their satisfaction with the quality of supervision, their satisfaction with the degree of challenge in their jobs, their internal work motivation, and the strength of their perceived need for individual growth. Findings, discussed at length, were based on responses from 207 teachers and showed that these classroom teachers saw their profession as intrinsically motivating, fulfilling, and satisfying and as a career to which they could make a life-long commitment. Teacher motivation can be supported by restructuring the job of teaching to allow for a greater degree of challenge and a greater outlet for the need to achieve, to advance, and to become self-actualized. References are included.

273. Frase, L.F. (1987). Is there a sound rationale behind the merit pay craze? *Teacher Education Quarterly, 14* (2), 90-100.

Merit pay proponents make these three claims: 1) merit pay will attract a higher caliber individual to teaching; 2) merit pay will help retain good teachers; 3) merit pay will motivate teachers to improve their instructional abilities. Using monetary incentives to compete with industry is an unlikely proposition. Internal rewards inherent in teaching are documented as the primary reason for people entering the teaching profession. The California Roundtable on Educational Opportunities found that the reasons for entering teaching could be grouped into two categories: 1) altruistic motives; 2) practical motives such as decent salary, job security, time off. So higher pay would probably be more important to industry managers than to school managers because the school managers don't choose educational work for the money.

274. George, P.S. (1987). Performance management in education. *Educational Leadership, 44* (7), 32, 34-39.

The author outlines a ten step model of performance management from corporate and government practices for use in teaching appraisal. These steps are:
1. build and maintain rapport,
2. focus on performance,
3. identify key result areas,
4. weight the key result areas,
5. jointly determine specific objectives,
6. assess performance levels,
7. monitor performance,
8. progress reviews,
9. the performance management interview,
10. follow-up.

275. Hoko, J. (1988). Merit pay-in search of the pedagogical widget. *Clearing House, 62* (1), 29-31.

The idea of merit pay is often thought of as a new idea. As early as the middle of the nineteenth century, payment-by-results existed as a policy for teachers in English and Welsh schools. In this country for eight decades, merit pay systems have been adopted and abandoned. They have failed mainly because of the inability to agree on functional units of measuring teacher merit. Attempts to determine the effectiveness of teachers have been futile.

Although attractive as a political lever, true merit pay systems remain fictional. Before we can evaluate good teaching, we must come to know what good teaching is; there is no best model. We must first determine the skills to be taught; then we can create an appropriate assessment. According to Hoko, teacher improvement more than merit pay is the most likely source of a real solution to the shortcomings of American schools.

276. Johns, H. (1988). Faculty perceptions of a teacher career ladder. *Contemporary Education, 59* (4), 198-203.

Merit pay has many proponents and opponents. This article researches the perception of teachers toward the career ladder program instituted in Tennessee in 1984. In essence, the plan is intended to reward the most competent teachers with higher positions and higher pay. The survey represents teacher attitudes after one full year's operation of the career ladder program.

277. Johnston, G.S. & Venable, B.P. (1986). A study of teacher loyalty to the principal: Rule administration and hierarchical influence of the principal. *Educational Administration Quarterly, 22* (4), 4-27.

This article discusses the relationship among principals' behavior in administering regulations, their hierarchical influence, and teacher loyalty to principals. Results of the study implied that there was a significant relationship found between rule behavior of secondary principals and teacher loyalty. Teacher loyalty for both secondary and elementary principals was related to hierarchical influence.

278. Jorde-Bloom, P. (1988). Teachers need "TLC" too. *Young Children, 43* (6), 4-8.

This article states that there are ten dimensions of climate which should be considered when trying to create a positive environment for teachers. They include:
   1. collegiality,
   2. professional growth,
   3. supervisor support,
   4. clarity of roles and policies,
   5. reward system,
   6. decision-making structure,
   7. goal consensus,
   8. task orientation,
   9. physical setting,
   10. innovativeness.

On the subject of collegiality, the author states that schools with a strong sense of it have a unified team spirit, people are comfortable, and express their thoughts openly.

279. Koll, P. J., et al. (1989). Collaboration between staff developers and school principals to promote professional growth. *Journal of Staff Development, 10* (3), 54-61.

This article reports results from a study of Wisconsin teachers and principals who were surveyed to identify factors which motivate teachers and principals to engage in continuing professional development.

280. Krupp, J.A. (1986). Using the power of the principalship to motivate experienced teachers. *Journal of Staff Development, 7* (2), 100-111.

This article describes how principals can learn about their teachers' developmental needs and use this information for creative staff development.

281. Lieberman, A. (1988). Teachers and principals: Turf, tension, and new tasks. *Phi Delta Kappan,* 648-653.

The author examines that schools have been organized and run in the same way as long as anyone can remember. She raises questions regarding how schools are run, who will share in running them, and in whose interest the schools will function. It is agreed that the teacher/student relationship is the heart of any attempt to restructure the schools. But all (principals, teachers, and students) seem likely to gain from schools that are structured to work better for the students and the adults. This idea raises many questions regarding how time is allotted, how resources can be organized, how teachers can work and learn together, how principals can facilitate collegiality, what new skills teachers will need, how teachers can be recognized in their own schools and districts, how professional development can be organized to meet local needs, and what new organizational forms might come into being.

282. Litt, M.D., & Turk, D.C. (1985). Sources of stress and dissatisfaction in experienced high school teachers. *Journal of Educational Research, 78* (3), 178-185.

The authors reported and discussed their findings of a survey of high school teachers which attempted to identify sources of stress and job dissatisfaction. Data was collected regarding perceived roles, school climate, coping resources, and specific work problems. Among several conclusions, the authors state that teachers feel uncertain about how they are perceived by supervisors and feel unable to exert any control over decisions which concern them. Teachers who feel comfortable with their principal and feel that they are interested in them on a personal and professional basis are more satisfied with their job.

283. Mickler, M.L. (1987). Merit pay: Boon or boondoggle? *Clearing House, 61* (3), 137-141.

Soon after the release of "A Nation At Risk," ex-President Reagan called for the adoption of merit pay policies that would compensate teachers for their classroom performance. Despite the success of some merit pay plans during the past 75 years, many more plans have failed than have succeeded.

Mickler speculates that past failures of merit pay systems suggest that there are fundamental problems that cannot be overcome by resolve and persistence. Further the author believes that educational reform is needed in American public schools. However, only time will tell whether merit pay will be instrumental in solving current educational problems.

284. Miller, R. (1985). An alternative proposal. *Phi Delta Kappan, 67*
      (2), 112.

Miller is a proponent of merit pay who believes that good work
should be rewarded. Miller suggests developing a form of incentive
reimbursement in state funding formulas. The author specifies that many
merit pay plans have failed because they lacked a workable plan, depended
on funds that came from other staff members, and required too much paper
work.

However, Miller states that success toward reform in education
depends on the ability of educational leaders to enable teachers to teach
better than ever before. Setting realistic outcomes and identifying
productive teachers can help to administer merit pay based on measurable
evidence.

285. Mills, H. (1987). Motivating your staff to excellence: Some
      considerations. *NASSP Bulletin,* 37-40.

Research in the past 20 years has shed some new light upon our
thinking regarding motivation. It shows that motivation is an internally
generated action where people act according to their needs and drives.
Based upon Maslow's Hierarchy of Needs the author offers a contingency
theory of motivation which includes five factors: (1) teacher motivational
levels, (2) motivational tools available to the motivator, (3) the situation,
(4) the credibility of the motivator, and (5) the dissatisfaction factor.
Principals must effectively motivate teachers to reach for higher levels of
excellence. Although this is a complex process, there are some steps to
help achieve it.

286. Mitchell, D.E. & Peters, M.J. (1988). A stronger profession
      through appropriate teacher incentives. *Educational Leadership, 46*
      (3), 74-78.

A primary goal of teacher-focused reform policies is enhanced work
motivation. What sort of reward system can be used to increase
motivation? It is recognized that the best rewards for good teaching are
intrinsic and symbolic rather than extrinsic and material. Teachers take a
sense of pride in student achievement and working with students. Material
benefits are no compensation for distasteful working conditions, a sense
of hopelessness in the schools or uncooperative students. An effective
incentive system emerges only when motivational goals are clearly
identified, an adequate supply of rewards is available and a reliable system
links the rewards to the goals.

287. Murname, R.J., & Cohen, D.K. (1986). Merit pay and the evaluation problem: Why most merit pay plans fail and a few survive. *Harvard Educational Review, 56* (1), 1-17.

Merit pay is often suggested as a way to provide strong incentive for employees to pursue organizational goals. The promise of merit pay is dimmed by its history. Most attempts to implement it have failed. Problems in school districts caused by merit pay have led many districts to drop merit pay plans. Merit pay tends to interfere with principals' efforts to build effective instructional teams. With merit pay, principals have to be more objective and in some cases this seems to discourage teachers.

288. Norton, M.S. & Hegebush, W.W. (1988). Incentive pay programs: Does participation change viewpoints? *Clearing House, 62* (4), 149-151.

The authors examine whether incentive pay programs influence the attitudes of school principals, central office administrators, school board members, and teachers. The ability of incentive pay to affect positively such factors as teacher motivation, quality of instruction, public respect for teachers, and the recruitment and retention of teachers were analyzed.

289. Ornstein, A. (1988). The changing status of the teacher profession. *Urban Education, 23* (3), 26-269.

Several trends are affecting teachers that have long-range repercussions in the profession, one of which is merit pay. Government officials, borrowing from principles used in the free enterprise system, have proposed that "Master Teachers" be identified and paid higher salaries. Some school boards think that merit pay as a supplement to base salary is an effective method of motivating teachers and encouraging excellence.

Both the NEA and AFT have reservations about merit pay, questioning whether objective performance standards can be implemented. Both fear that merit pay will lead to politics and patronage. They are afraid that teachers who don't comply with bureaucratic mandates will be penalized and the unity of teachers will be threatened. Many educators think that competition for pay would reduce cooperation among educators. There is also evidence that intrinsic rewards, not financial incentives, are prime motivators for teachers.

290. Peach, L.E. & Reddick, T L. (1989). *A study to assess school climate within the public schools of the central geographic region of Tennessee.* (Eric Document Reproduction Service No. ED 317 334).

The authors indicate that a positive school climate is an important factor in school effectiveness. In this paper the authors review the major determinants of school climate and also report the findings of a survey of 246 teachers and 76 principals in rural public schools in central Tennessee concerning three school climate factors: motivation and morale; communications; and leadership. Over 40% of the teachers stated that the climate in their schools "almost never" made them enthusiastic about their work or instilled professional pride in themselves or other staff.

291. Richardson, G.D., & Sistrunk, W.E. (1989). *The relationship between secondary teachers' perceived levels of burnout and their perceptions of their principals' supervisory behaviors.* (Eric Document Reproduction Service No. ED 312 763).
      This study investigated differences in teachers' perceptions of their burnout levels and their perceptions of their principals' supervisory behaviors. Results indicated that teachers' perceptions of their burnout levels and their perceptions of the principals' supervisory behaviors were positively related. Teachers who perceived their own levels of emotional exhaustion to be low also perceived their principals as nondirective. Teachers who did feel burned out perceived their principals as directive.

292. Rosenholtz, S.J. (1986). Career ladders and merit pay: Capricious fads or fundamental reforms? *The Elementary School Journal, 86* (4), 513-527.
      Proponents of merit pay advance several arguments: (1) monetary incentives will motivate teachers to excel; (2) monetary incentives will retain good teachers; (3) merit pay will attract better candidates into teaching; and (4) merit pay will keep good teachers in the classroom rather than going into administration. Teachers rarely consider salary a rewarding aspect of their work; they value intrinsic, psychic rewards that come from student growth and development and from confidence in their own ability to help students. Monetary incentives do not persuade teachers to stay in schools where psychic rewards of their work do not outweigh the frustrations. Most merit pay plans carry a length-of-appointment prerequisite, i.e. longevity. Problems of merit pay include: how to determine objetive standards for teacher evaluation and how to promote quality teaching. Teachers are often unclear about how they are doing, leaving the teachers unrewarded and without specific information they need for improvement. Merit pay plans tend to lower teacher morale.

293. Rossmiller, R.A. (1984). *Changing educational practice through continuing professional development programs.* (Eric Document Reproduction Service No. ED 249 609).

Research on effective schools has shown the important role of the school principal in encouraging and supporting the continuing professional development of teachers. It is clear that professional development activities designed to improve the knowledge and skill of teachers already in service represents an effective means of changing educational practice and, in turn, the learning and achievement of students.

Research supports the conclusion that teachers are motivated to participate in continuing professional development activities primarily by intrinsic factors. However, too little attention is paid to this when designing professional development to enhance their performance.

294. Schlansker, B. (1987). A principal's guide to teacher stress. *Principal, 66* (5), 32-34.

In this article the author states that the principal plays an important role in helping teachers deal with stress. She states that seven supports were identified in her research, which are:
1. sharing professional experiences,
2. getting administrative support on policy,
3. access to support personnel,
4. receiving feedback on teaching performance from principal,
5. principal showing actions of sharing, caring, and interacting,
6. job security,
7. provision of adequate physical facilities.

The article includes an inventory which the author asserts determined what supports were important in combatting stress.

295. Sergiovanni, T.J. & Moore, J.H. (1989). *School for tomorrow.* MA: Allan & Bacon.

The authors argue that until the average teacher's salary is equivalent to the average college graduate's salary, any effort to provide salary rewards to teachers on any basis that is not uniformly accessible to all teachers will cause morale problems. If teachers feel that their occupational choice prevents them equal access to rewards available to other college graduates, they will resist differentiation among themselves. People who share a feeling of disadvantage place a greater value on commonality than on opportunities for a few to escape that status.

296. Shanker, A. (1985). Separating wheat from chaff. *Phi Delta Kappan, 67* (2), 108-109.

Shanker would like to see the merit pay issue put to rest because he believes merit pay is a major barrier to the teaching profession. Further, he speculates that merit pay is not an incentive plan to improve teaching knowledge or skills because it means principals and supervisors evaluate and attempt to standardize teacher behavior by using inadequate check lists. Some teachers are rewarded and others are demoralized, often on the basis of favoritism or politics. Teachers become competitive with each other in an unhealthy way; it is difficult for them to strive together for school excellence. Teachers have continued to oppose merit pay because no system has met the criteria of being able to identify and reward outstanding teachers and yet create incentive for all teachers to improve.

297. Stedt, J.D. & Fraser, H.W. (1984). A checklist for improving teacher morale. *NASSP Bulletin, 68* (470), 70-81.

This article describes a Behavioral Morale Checklist which defines morale in terms of observable behavior. It includes recommendations for principals to improve morale.

298. Trubowitz, S. (1978). The principal helps improve reading instruction. *Reading Horizons, 18* (3), 186-189.

In this article the author demonstrates how principals can strengthen school reading programs through recognizing their role as instructional leaders, stressing reading as a priority goal, implementing change with sensitivity and skill, and developing an in-service program which provides teachers with support, structure, and stimulation.

299. Walker, J.E. (1990). The skills of exemplary principals. *NASSP Bulletin, 74* (524), 48-55.

NASSP's Assessment Center Project has identified 12 key skills for successful principals: problem analysis, judgement, organizational ability, decisiveness, leadership, sensitivity, stress tolerance, oral communication, written communication, wide-ranging interests, personal motivation, and educational values. Principals help others to improve by motivation.

300. Weller, L.D. (1982). Principals, meet Maslow: A prescription for teacher retention. *NASSP Bulletin, 66* (456), 32-36.

Weller states in this article that principals should use Maslow's hierarchy of basic human needs in dealing with teachers. The author reasons that this would create a more favorable school climate, which in turn would allow teachers to perform at their best.

The author takes each of the six human needs: physiological, safety and security, love and affiliation, esteem, knowledge and understanding, and self-actualization in turn and tries to demonstrate its applicability to teachers.

It shows some examples of how, by meeting these needs, principals can affect the morale, not only of the teachers, but the entire school.

301. Wentworth, M. (1990). Developing Staff Morale. *The Practitioner, 16* (4).
Low staff morale often results from professional lives that have little meaning. It can also result from frustration and the inability to change what is happening and from muddled goals and demands exceeding scarce resources. Principals are responsible for responding to daily human concerns, for understanding scheduling demands, and for fostering recognition programs, staff meetings, shared leadership, good communication, and professional development.

CHAPTER 18

Sensitivity

Principals in twenty-first century schools must exhibit sensitivity to a variety of constituents. Sensitivity means more than respecting another person's opinion or position. For principals, sensitivity means the ability to empathize with "all kinds of people" (Thomson, 1990, p. 2). Several of the most obvious constituencies include minorities, females, students, faculty, and subordinates.

MINORITIES

Recent research indicates that the demographics of America are changing rapidly. In fact, some speculate that by 2010 the ethnic make-up of the country will almost reverse. Although some would argue that more ethnically diverse principals are needed in the schools, current and future principals must also be sensitive to the needs, perceptions, and expectations of minority students, faculty, and community members (Sleeter & Grant, 1988). Principals can demonstrate sensitivity by providing appropriate role models for students by building culturally diversity in the makeup of faculty (Bey, 1992).

GENDER ISSUES

The majority of teachers are female but most administrators are male. Principals should be sensitive to the needs and aspirations of female students and faculty members. For example, very few elementary teachers are male, but more should be employed. Likewise, more females should be employed as administrators if they have the appropriate qualifications (Mertz & McNeely, 1991).

JUSTIFICATION

Many of the educational reforms of the past decade have been promoted to improve learning opportunities for students. However, in implementation, most reform has done little to change the welfare of students. Eisner (1990) has speculated that many of the educational reforms have the wrong purpose; that the reforms are not aimed at preparing students for life, but for scoring well on a standardized test. Gardner (1962) proposed that we have constructed a narrow view of excellence which examines only native ability. He postulated that in reality schools should embrace achievement of many kinds and at various levels, and that students should be recognized for differences in talent not differences in human worth.

Principals must also be sensitive to students' environments. Corrigan (1992) reports that "more than 12 million American children, the equivalent of half the population of Canada, are now poor" (p. 35). Corrigan (1992) continues that "by designing schools that are unresponsive to the disadvantaged . . . the American education system is just producing an uneducated work force" (p. 35). Levin (1985) suggests that additional time in school and increased educational standards are likely to increase the dropout rates. Principals, then, need to be sensitive to the educational and cultural background of their students.

SUBORDINATES

Principals need to be sensitive to co-workers, particularly assistant principals. In many other professions, the responsibility of middle managers is to train their replacements. In education, middle managers, principals, are often hesitant to share responsibility and authority with subordinates. Principals need to be more sensitive to the needs of assistant principals and help prepare them to assume a principalship. Most often, the assistant principalship is a "stepping stone," not a permanently desired position (Golanda, 1991). Consequently, principals should assist them in their professional development.

NOTES

Bey, T.M. (1992). Multicultural teacher development: Diversifying approaches for improvement. *Kappa Delta Pi Record, 28* (2), 59–62.

Corrigan, D.C. (1992). Reinventing the American school. *Kappa Delta Pi Record, 28* (2), 35–41.

Eisner, E. (1990). What's the purpose of school? *Update of the Association for Supervision and Curriculum Development, 32* (10), 4.

Gardner, J. (1962). *Excellence: Can we be equal and excellent, too?* New York: Harper.

Golanda, G.L. (1991). Preparing tomorrow's educational leaders: An inquiry regarding the wisdom of utilizing the position of assistant principal as an internship or apprenticeship to prepare future principals. *Journal of School Leadership, 1* (3), 266–283.

Levin, H.M. (1985). *The educationally disadvantaged: A national crisis.* Philadelphia, PA: Public Private Ventures.

Mertz, N.T., & McNeely, S.R. (1991). Male and female professors of educational administrators: A view from within. *Journal of School Leadership, 1* (4), 363–378.

Sleeter, C.E., & Grant, C.A. (1988). *Making choices for multicultural education: Five approaches to race, color, and gender.* Columbus, OH: Merrill.

Thomson, S.D. (1990). New framework for preparing principals developed by National Commission for the Principalship. (News release). Fairfax, VA: National Commission for the Principalship.

BIBLIOGRAPHY

302. Blase, J.J., & Williams, H.B. (1987). Politics in the school: Teachers' political orientations toward the principal. *Journal of Humanistic Education and Development, 26* (2), 72–80.

An investigation of political behaviors in the teacher-principal relationship from the teachers' perspective using unstructured and semistructured interviews demonstrated that the political perspective of the teachers was based on sensitivity to the power of principals and the development of strategies to deal with power in protecting themselves from and influencing the behaviors of their school principals.

303. Funk, C. (1986). *The female executive in school administration: profiles, pluses, and problems.* (Eric Document Reproduction Service No. ED 285 282)

Successful women administrators in public schools can provide valuable information concerning the advantages and disadvantages of being a "female executive." The author describes a study of 66 female public school executives in the Texas metroplex area. Common problems identified by the respondents included difficulty in gaining male respect and acceptance, no entry to the male network, lack of "authority" and trust (from female employees), and employment discrimination.

304. Johnson, M.C., & Rex, D J. (1984). *The impact of principals' assessment centers on career opportunities for women.* (Eric Document Reproduction Service No. ED 300 881)

Historically, women have been underrepresented in public school administrative positions, largely due to sex role and occupational stereotyping. This study examines how National Association of Secondary School Principals (NASSP) assessment centers influenced women's career opportunities, how these women view the process, and what issues face women aspiring to be principals. By late 1983, 624 women had been evaluated at the centers. In this study, survey instruments were sent to the 549 women whose addresses were known with a response rate of 60 percent. Of the 332 respondents, 82 have received promotions since their NASSP evaluation. A majority indicated that assessment center results were either totally or partially responsible for their promotion, while 22 percent do not perceive assessment as influencing their promotion, and 12 percent do not know the effect of these results. Demographic differences (age, race, and marital status) did not appear to influence promotion decisions.

305. Kaser, J.S. (1985). *Guidelines for enhancing participation in mixed gender work groups.* (ED 294 996)

This guide is intended to help principals, department chairs, teachers, and other educators who are chairing a mixed gender work group. The first section discusses research-identified differences between the way men and women communicate (both verbally and nonverbally) in groups. A 23-item gender communications assessment, which is designed to assess the extent to which the men and women in a particular group are communicating (both verbally and nonverbally) is provided. The guide also contains thirteen strategies for reducing verbal communication barriers, three for reducing nonverbal communication barriers, and four for reducing both verbal and nonverbal communication barriers. Sample situations that group leaders may encounter in mixed gender work groups and sample responses to the situation are also presented.

306. Miskel, C., & Cosgrove, D. (1984). Leader succession: A model and review for school settings. (Eric Document Reproduction Service No. ED 242 066).

In the public school, the replacement of principals or superintendents is disruptive. It changes lines of communication, realizes relationships of power, and disturbs the process of normal activities. One of the goals of this paper was to suggest a variety of strategies to examine administrative succession as well as effects of leaders on school processes and outcomes.

The authors are in agreement that the truly critical phenomena occur before the leader comes on the scene and immediately after arrival. It is during the pre- and post-arrival phases that arguments for resource allocations, goals and performance, and job responsibilities are redefined. Administrator effectiveness, therefore, will be more visible during this relatively unstable period. "Change," through succession, is important to formal organizations and their leadership.

307. Panyako, D., & Rorie, L. (1987). The changing role of the assistant principal. *NASSP Bulletin, 71* (501), 6–8.

Although often overlooked in significance and prestige, the assistant principal is perhaps the most changing feature of the school today. If the "principal" is viewed as chief executive officer, the assistant principal becomes invisible; recognition and prestige, therefore, become invisible as well.

This perception is changing, however, and a new breed of assistant principal is entering administration. The office now involves many responsibilities and technical tasks that require special knowledge and training. Today's assistant principal must be knowledgeable in all aspects of school management, from financial accounting, law, and psychological measurement to staff supervision and evaluation and effective communication techniques.

The dynamic assistant principal must aspire to the principalship, which sometimes depends on how much responsibility the principal is willing to share. Also, this may depend on attitudes in the central office. Although the assistant principal was originally hired to free the principal of administrative and management details, today's more complex societal demands necessitate a redefining of the assistant principal, thus ensuring a more productive and accountable school administrator.

308. Schulte, S.L. (1988). The woman educational administrator is both the ideal and reality. *Education, 109* (2), 152–154.

Once in the seat of power, do women have the capabilities to handle the job? Are women as competent as men in the field of administration? Women are, in fact, often hired to fill quotas and affirmative action policies. Yet many surpass the minimum qualifications often required. Women must overcome stereotypic biases that block their paths. For example, the notion that women administrators are either "old maids" or tough, masculine females who pushed their way to the top are stereotypes that may still exist today.

The composite portrait of a good administrator, be it male or female, includes the following characteristics: well-organized; attends to detail; warm, caring, and relates well to people; sees the "big picture"; delegates authority without relinquishing it; allows others to grow and reach potential; forms judgement after listening to all sides of an issue; has a sense of humor; and is ultimately professional.

309. Sheive, L.T., & Schoenheit, M.B. (1987). *Leadership: Examining the elusive.* 1987 Yearbook of the Association for Supervision and Curriculum Development. Arlington, VA: ASCD.

A compilation of works by various authors, the focus of this book is on leadership in educational organizations. The guiding concepts are symbolic leadership and culture, with an integrating frame of reference suggested by the study: vision, goals, climate, monitoring, and intervention.

310. Smith, J.A. (1987). Assistant principals: New demands, new realities, and new perspectives. *NASSP Bulletin, 71* (501), 9–12.

The author, an assistant principal in Seattle, Washington, conducted a research study to determine the following: (1) the background of selected assistant principals; (2) experiences their superiors feel are essential for promotion; (3) stated differences between assistant principals in urban, suburban, and rural districts; and (4) perceptions of district superintendents regarding assistant principals.

To summarize the author's findings: (1) current duties have changed drastically from the 1960s; (2) assistant principals are happiest in their jobs when involved with curriculum and instruction, student activities, teacher personnel, professional development, and school management; (3) assistant principals want to be perceived not so much as disciplinarians, but as educational leaders; and (4) school districts should seek ways to assign the less meaningful tasks to other personnel.

311. West, E.L. (1978). The co-principalship: Administrative realism. *High School Journal, 61* (5), 241–246.

Given the expectations of the board of education, teachers, parents, and students, secondary school administrators face increasingly high levels of frustration. The author proposes a workable alternative: The establishment of a "co-principalship." Instead of a principal and several assistant principals, the co-principalship allows for one administrator to become the "principal for instruction" while the other becomes the "principal for administration." Each has specific job objectives and responsibilities.

Job descriptions and responsibilities are designed to maximize efficiency of the total school program. Roles of other assistants, such as dean of students, would be modified.

At the end of the first year of operation, data revealed that this concept works for school districts who are looking for more productive means of accomplishing objectives. The author observed the following significant features of the program's evaluation:

— Increased number of class visits and follow-ups
— Reduction in suspensions and expulsions
— Increased participation of staff in in-service
— Increased cleanliness of school
— Increased efficiency of the custodial staff
— Greater job satisfaction for administrators.

CHAPTER 19

Oral Communication

Oral communication is a dynamic process that undergirds virtually all human activity. Communication permeates organization, leadership, structure, and the motivation and decision making by allowing people to discuss the processes. According to Hoy and Miskel (1991) "communication permeates every aspect of school life" (p. 343).

WHO IS INVOLVED?

Oral communication involves at least two people, the sender and the receiver. In schools, oral communication is unavoidable because teachers and principals earn their living by talking and listening (Smith, 1966). Therefore, oral communication can be defined as dialogue. Dialogue means that everyone has had experiences that may cloud their perception of reality. In oral communication, perception is reality. The perception of the receiver of a message is the reality of the message, not the intended message of the sender. Good oral communication requires the sender to check perceptions occasionally to make sure the messages are clear and accurate. There are numerous techniques and instruments which principals can use for this purpose.

LISTENING

Listening is a critical element of oral communication but one that is seldom practiced. Good listeners are good communicators. Principals should practice good listening skills and understand that non-verbal communication (body language, etc.) is a vital part of good listening.

CONFLICT

Conflict is a reality of human existence. There are natural tensions between individuals as communication takes place. But these tensions are normal, healthy, and promote growth of the communicators and the organization (Hanson & Lifton, 1991). Conflicting points of view are evident in all walks of life, particularly education. Most people understand that conflict is inevitable. However, some shy away from conflict and, in so doing, eliminate a tremendous opportunity to increase their knowledge of another individual, a group, or the organization. Conflict should not necessarily be encouraged, but neither should it be totally avoided.

WHY IS ORAL COMMUNICATION UNIQUE?

"Man is the only creature who can talk himself into trouble, but he is also the only creature who by talking things over can find a way out of trouble" (Royal Bank of Canada, 1969, p. 1). If education is to improve, principals must learn to use oral communication in more effective and efficient ways. Talking "at" someone is not the same as talking "with" someone. Teachers, parents, and students desire honest communication, not authoritative speech making. Dialogue is the language of communication, monologue in the language of egotism. Dialogue is constructive because it adds to knowledge; monologue is destructive because it indicates fear.

SUCCESSFUL ORAL COMMUNICATION

Hanson and Lifton (1991) discuss three principles of effective communication: (1) depend upon and build trust; (2) make information public, both known and unknown; and (3) have open relationship between sender and receiver on content and purpose of communication.

SUMMARY

Principals must use effective oral communication to be successful; their livelihood depends on it.

NOTES

Hanson, J.H., & Lifton, E. (1991). *School restructuring: A practitioner's guide*. Swampscott, MA: Watersun Publishing Company.

Hoy, W.K., & Miskel, C.G. (1991). *Educational administration: Theory, research, and practice*. New York: McGraw-Hill.

Smith, A.G. (1966). *Communication and culture*. New York: Holt, Rinehart, & Winston.

The Royal Bank of Canada. (1969, August). Time to talk things over. *The Royal Bank of Canada Monthly Letter*, 50 (8), 1–4.

BIBLIOGRAPHY

312. Bloom, B.S. (1986, February). Automaticity: "The hands and feet of genius." *Educational Leadership, 43* (5), 70–77.

Bloom identified communication skills as being learned to the level of automaticity. These skills are rarely thought about in relationship to the set of intended responses. While engaged in conversation or in writing, the words come to us as we talk or write.

Prerequisite skills for a life of change could be the development of processes and skills found in group dynamics, problem solving, time management, organizational development, and strategic planning.

313. Bromberg, M. (1975). Principal William Shakespeare. *NASSP Bulletin, 59* (393), 78–82.

This writer suggests some Shakespearian gems for dealing with everyone from reporters to superintendents. You can try your old-time memorization techniques on these apropos utterances—and be prepared for anything.

314. Forsyth, P.B., & Boshart, D. (1985). *Leadership style and principal communication: A preliminary investigation.* (ERIC Document Reproduction Service No. ED 263 644)

The need for further research was indicated by the results of a limited exploration of the concept that principals' communications with teachers mediate between the principals' leadership styles and the effectiveness of the organizations they head. Twenty-seven Kansas elementary principals of schools with student populations between 215 and 315 were asked to complete Fiedler's Least Preferred Co-worker scale to determine their leadership styles. Three principals were selected from each of the style groups identified: those who were relationship-oriented, those who were task-oriented, and those dominated by neither orientation. These principals then completed the Norton Communicator Style Measure. The teachers serving under the principals completed the Communication Satisfaction Survey. Tape recordings were made of the principals' oral communications with teachers. The relationship-oriented principals saw themselves as relaxed, open, and easy-going, but their teachers were dissatisfied and they communicated least of the three groups. The principals without dominant orientation communicated most frequently, particularly concerning issues of control, but teachers were not very satisfied. Task-oriented principals focused on instructions and on personal talk and left teachers more satisfied. The results suggested that leadership style is manifested in observable behavior, but were not intended to be conclusive.

315. Heuss, R., & Psencik, K. (1986). *Aiming for administrative excellence. Appraising principals: A proposed model.* (ERIC Document Reproduction Service No. ED 297 416)

If principals are responsible for implementing educational reforms, then criteria for effective leadership skills should be developed. This paper considers criteria for identifying effective principals and proposes a training and appraisal system. The paper discusses five domains that identify effective principals: (1) vision, (2) organization/collaboration, (3) people skills, (4) communication skills, and (5) hardiness. The proposed Administrator Improvement Model (AIM) is instructionally designed to develop effective leadership skills. Training involves classroom activities, role-playing situations, and self- and peer evaluation/coaching.

316. Hogue, J. (1987). Improved conference skills: Focus on communication strengths. *NASSP Bulletin, 71* (503), 56–60.

The key to holding successful administrator-teaching conferences is effective communication. Administrators must recognize the strengths of their teachers and be able to capitalize on them. The success of communication depends upon the supervisor's ability to analyze and appeal to the natural strengths of another individual, and to utilize his or her natural strengths.

The ability to reflect, probe, support and advise are essential skills for an effective supervisor. An effective conference will provide feedback that is of value to both individuals and deliver a message in such a way that it will be received and acted upon. Thus, knowing yourself and the other person, and utilizing that information in the interaction, is the key to a successful conference.

BI/POLAR psychology is an effective tool to sensitive awareness and equips the supervisor with these skills. The basic principle of this theory of psychology asserts that a cluster of positive strengths exists within every person. The BI/POLAR system approaches communication from a positive and affirming perspective.

317. Lucietto, L.L. (1970). Speech patterns of administrators. *Administrator's Notebook, 18* (5), 1–4.

Results of this study of 20 elementary school principals indicate a relationship between the language usage of school administrators and the intensity of certain characteristics in their administrative behavior.

318. Maidment, R. (1987). How do you rate me as a listener? *NASSP Bulletin, 71* (499), 87–91.

Listening, our most frequently used sense, is our most neglected communication skill. The three-fourths listening law prevails in educational settings: three-fourths of our day is consumed by talking and listening activity; three-fourths of whatever we hear, we hear imprecisely; and three-fourths of what we hear accurately, we forget within three weeks.

This article includes a listening inventory that can be taken as a self-appraisal and would be a far more effective tool with someone rating another. (Example: teachers rate the principal).

This inventory would be an excellent evaluation tool which can be used individually or in any type of setting.

319.   Neill, S.B. (1983). *How to communicate effectively with staff members: Tips for principals from NASSP.* (ERIC Document Reproduction Service No. ED 240 680)

Recommendations for improving communications skills are offered. It is stated that the process of communicating involves passing information and understanding from one person to another; a one-way process of sending out information is not good enough. To help principals communicate more effectively with their staff, recommendations are offered on the following topics: (1) improving listening skills; (2) making sure that the message is getting through to the other person; and (3) deciding whether to use oral or written communication. A list of reasons why misunderstandings occur is also included.

320.   Valentine, J.W., et al. (1975). Administrative verbal behavior: What you say does make a difference. *NASSP Bulletin, 59* (395), 67–74.

Verbal interaction with the various segments of school and community is the principal's most time consuming and important activity. This article reports a study of how verbal expression can affect a school's climate.

321.   Wiles, K., & Lovell, J.T. (1975). *Supervision for better schools.* Englewood Cliffs, NJ: Prentice-Hall.

A person can be more effective in communication if he recognizes some of the most common difficulties people encounter in seeking to understand each other.

1. People use symbols or words that have different meanings.
2. Members of the group have different values.
3. Different perceptions of the problems.
4. Emphasis on status.
5. Conflict in interest.

6. Making decisions by the majority vote rather than seeking consensus.
7. Attempts to keep feelings out of the discussion.
8. Use of words to prevent thinking.
9. Lack of desire to understand the other person's point of view or his feelings or his values or his purposes.
10. Lack of acceptance of diversity.
11. A one-way concept of cooperation.
12. Feelings of superiority.
13. Vested interests.
14. Feelings of personal insecurity.
15. An obvious attempt to sell.
16. The concepts that the sender and the receiver have of their roles.
17. Negative feelings about the situation.

CHAPTER 20

Written Communication

For the principal of the twenty-first century, effective written communication skills are critical. People inside and outside the organization judge principals by the way communications are handled: the way principals write, and the quality of their writing.

BACKGROUND

Colleagues and clientele have the opportunity to review written communications, check the spelling, grammar, structure and, often, the content of the communications. Written communications lead to a sense of permanence; they are not easily erased, and they are available for others to inspect, analyze, and evaluate. The image of the principal and the school is at stake when written communications are involved, particularly when communication rules are violated. After all, schools teach communication skills and to see poorly written communication rules modeled by the leader of the school is almost inexcusable.

LIMITATIONS OF WRITTEN COMMUNICATION

A major limitation of written communication is the inability of the receiver of the communication to provide feedback to the sender; the words stand in silent testimony to the isolation of written communication. Typically, feedback is provided after the receiver of the communication has the opportunity to read the written message and make an analysis of the written words. Oral communication permits the sender to "read" the audience and make adjustments in the message accordingly, but such is not the case in written communication. Consequently, written communication forces the sender to meticulously examine each word in the message to assure clear, concise, and convincing language.

IMPORTANCE OF WRITTEN COMMUNICATION

Written communication is important for five reasons:

1. The writer is judged by the communication.
2. Written communication does not allow immediate feedback.
3. Selecting the appropriate word to convey the appropriate meaning is difficult.
4. Written communication is permanent.
5. Written communication can be analyzed and judged.

STAGES OF WRITTEN COMMUNICATION

Quattrini (1986) specifies four states in written communication:

1. the pre-writing or planning stage,
2. the composing/drafting/writing stage,
3. the revising and editing stage, and
4. the development of the final copy stage.

Many principals forget or purposefully leave out the third stage, which is critical to the success of written communication. The writer of the communication needs someone else to proofread and edit all material. For principals, a secretary, an assistant principal, an English teacher, etc. should proofread all written communication, particularly any going outside the building or the organization. Nothing makes a worse impression than grammatical errors in a written letter to a parent, the superintendent, etc.

Achilles and Norman (1974) propose seven key elements that will improve written communications:

1. unity,
2. purpose and consistency of purpose,
3. clarity and specificity,
4. accuracy and objectivity,
5. organization,

6. appropriateness, and
7. attention to mechanics.

PERCEPTIONS AND INTERPRETATIONS OF WRITTEN COMMUNICATION

Written communication demonstrates problems of perception and interpretation on the part of the receiver of the communication and problems of intent and skill of delivery on the part of the sender of the communication. However, written communication is vital to the effective operation of schools and to the efficiency of the principal in schools.

You must have an exceptional command of language. You're expected to be a model for your school community, so your written communications must be crisp, factual, and grammatically perfect. . . . Every time you communicate, you're on center stage; and you're under some pressure to give an eloquent, stimulating, precise, and grammatically correct performance (Heller, 1986, p. 54).

Remind yourself before you start writing, as you're writing, and as you review . . . that clarity is essential. The goal is communication, not obfuscation. Practice finding the simplest way of making each point. A few basics: use plain English, simple syntax, short sentences (Ficklen, 1986, p. 48).

COMMUNICATION AND LEADERSHIP

Hersey and Blanchard (1988) have identified three basic competencies of leadership, or the influencing of others, as diagnosing, adapting, and communicating. They define communications as "being able to put the message in a way that people can easily understand and accept" (p. 305). Other researchers agree: "the writer's responsibility is to communicate the message and make it easy for the reader" (Yerkes & Morgan, 1991, p. 2). If written communication helps form the basis for leadership, then principals need to model effective communication techniques. "Principals cannot afford to let poor writing get out the door. It may offend readers, create confusion, and limit the credibility of education as an enterprise, the school as an institution, and the leader as a professional" (Yerkes & Morgan, 1991, p. 8).

SUMMARY

"The main goal of the writer is to be understood. If we don't choose words that are concrete, specific, and in the reader's vocabulary, we fail; our message misses the mark" (Yerkes & Morgan, 1991, p. 12).

NOTES

Achilles, C.M., & Norman, D. (1974). Communication and change in education. *Planning and Changing, 5* (3), 138–142.

Ficklen, E. (1986). Writing a memo? Here is how to communicate—not obfuscate. In *Design your success*. Reston, VA: National School Boards Association.

Heller, R.W. (1986). Do you have what it takes to stand out from the crowd? In *Design your success*. Reston, VA: National School Boards Association, p. 47–49.

Quattrini, J. (1986). Take these five steps to chip away at writer's block. In *Design your success*. Reston, VA: National School Boards Association, p. 51–52.

BIBLIOGRAPHY

322.   Anderlini, L.S. (1983). An inservice program for improving team participation in educational decision-making. *School Psychology Review, 12* (2), 160–167.

Feedback is verbal and nonverbal communication that gives a person information on how his/her behavior affects another's perceptions. Feedback is also a reaction by others in their feeling and perceptions and how one's behavior affects others receiving feedback. This process can be shown through the Johari Window which was developed by Joseph Luft and Harry Ingham for use in group processes. This model is a communication window which illustrates information about the individual and others. Additional information on written communication is also important.

323.   Dublin, A. (1986). Administrators' conduits for cross cultural communication. *Thrust, 8* (1), 22–23.

According to all research there are multiple racial and ethnic backgrounds represented in the public school population. Administrators need good written communication skills in order to deal effectively with these students. Schools, as principals, must assume a leadership role to understand the differences between peoples and the complexities of their environments and communicate accurate information. Schools that enhance communication between foreign students and nationals (U.S. citizens) will benefit students and educators.

324.   Gotts, E., & Purnell, R. (1985). *Improving home school communication. (Phi Delta Kappan Fastback #230)*. Bloomington, IN: Phi Delta Kappa.

Home-school communications may be for groups of parents or for individuals. Group communications are used when schools need to share information widely about their program, activity schedule, accomplishments, and needs. Individual communications are used when contacting parents on matters of academic progress and needs of individual students. Four methods of communication are especially useful with groups of parents: newsletters, open house, handbooks, and parent organizations.

325.   Gougeon, T.D., et al. (1990). *A quantitative phenomenological study of leadership: Social control theory applied to actions of school principals*. (ERIC Document Reproduction Service No. ED 321 369)

The paper compares principals' self-perceptions of social control communication with teacher perceptions, including principals' communication patterns. Structural functionalist and symbolic interactionist theories are integrated with the leader as social control (LASC) model to develop an instrument to measure teachers' and principals' communication perceptions. The model is based on two variables, motivation and orientation. A shadowing technique utilizing qualitative data and a comparison of biographical and situational factors were used to collect the data.

Heuss, R., & Psencik, K. Cited above as item 315.

326. Kersting, T. (1984). Administrative jargon as a barrier to effective communication. *NASSP Bulletin, 68* (472), 97–99.

Speaking effectively is required in nearly all tasks and functions of supervision and is central to the communications systems of the school whether it takes the form of a friendly note or letter, bulletin, memo, report, or news release. Most administrators who use educational jargon are unaware that their use of language prevents clear, precise communication. Whether the linguistic obscurity is deliberate or not, administrators and supervisors could clearly benefit from study of fundamental communication skills.

327. Podsen, I.J. (1991). Apprehension and effective writing in the principalship. *NASSP Bulletin, 75* (532), 89–96.

The NASSP Assessment Center Program uses written communication as one of twelve indicators of success. In this study, a random sample of 305 principals was drawn from the membership rosters of four NASSP Principal Assessment Centers. Responses from 100 principals (33 percent) show that there is a relationship between writing apprehension level on performance of job writing skills. The author advises current and future school administrators to take courses in current written communication practices.

328. Wynn, R. (1985). Open communication. *The Practitioner, 11* (4), 3.

The author states that 90 percent of all human problems could be partly solved if the parties would take the time to talk and listen. Open communication is the key to solving conflict with students, teachers, and parents, but is not easily gained. Rules must be strictly enforced to achieve open communication during controversial discussions. These rules allow every speaker to express his/her feelings without being evaluated before the other party speaks.

329. Yerkes, D., & Morgan, S. (1991). *Strategies for success: An administrator's guide to writing*. Reston, VA: National Association of Secondary School Principals.

This monograph represents an invaluable resource to practicing or potential principals. The authors write in a clear and cogent manner, including numerous examples to illustrate their points. The book accurately models the author's stated purpose of increasing writing skills.

SECTION FIVE
CONTEXTUAL SKILLS

CHAPTER 21

Philosophical and Cultural Values

For years, archaeologists and anthropologists have studied the artifacts produced by alien, and sometimes ancient, cultures. The purpose of their study is to understand the culture that produced the artifacts, not simply to recreate the artifacts in modern society (Deal & Kennedy, 1982). Much of school reform, though, has been directed at recreating the artifacts of effective schools, rather than recreating the culture that produced those artifacts. For example, installing a new homework monitoring program in the school will not ensure quality educational outcomes, just as a new discipline code, which ensures order, will not necessarily produce better learning.

CULTURE

Webster's New Collegiate Dictionary (1988) calls culture "the integrated pattern of human behavior that includes thought, speech, action and artifacts, and depends on man's capacity for learning and transmitting knowledge to succeeding generations."

The American Heritage Dictionary says culture is "the totality of socially transmitted behavior patterns, arts, beliefs, institutions, and all other products of human word and thought characteristic of a community or population."

In both cases, it is clear that culture's effects are awesome; it defines the very way people think about phenomena and the way people behave. It even determines, to a large degree, what people will believe (and disbelieve) and how people will view the events of their lives. In simpler

219

form, Marvin Bower, in *The Will to Manage,* calls culture "the way we do things around here."

Whatever the definition, culture controls behavior to a large degree. And, because culture is inexorably linked with social interaction, it is not static; it can be changed by its members just as it changes them.

VALUES

Peters and Waterman (1982) have emphasized the importance of values in successful organizations. Deal and Kennedy (1982) not only points out the importance of these core values, but the critical means by which they are disseminated in a complex organization. Both of these works provide useful insights for school administrators who wish to create schools which display values that encourage excellence.

"Organizational values are the basic beliefs that control the way an institution operates" (Goodlad, 1984). For the most part, these values are obvious to everyone in the institution and pervade every activity the organization undertakes. They are the criteria by which one can judge the correctness of individual and collective behavior.

> Values are the bedrock of any institution. They articulate the essence of the organization's philosophy about how it goes about achieving success. They provide a sense of common direction and guidelines for everyday behavior. Most important, values tell what your organization stands for . . . what it thinks is important. (Goodlad, 1984, p. 27)

But values are not concrete like policies, rules, budgets, or curriculum guides. Often they are not even written down. They are, however, manifested in everything the school does because they guide the choices that are made—choices about content and method of teaching, choices about how schools spend their and their students' time, choices about who is rewarded and what gets rewarded.

What do effective schools value? What do they believe? By what values should principals try to shape their school?

There appears to be a cadre of values that are essential for institutional success, whether the institution is a business, a school, a government agency, or a recreational club. The content of these values is:

1. A belief in being the best there is.
2. A belief in the importance and value of individual people.

3. A belief in the importance of the details of the job; dedication to doing all parts of a job well.
4. A belief in providing superior service (or education).
5. A belief that most members of an organization should be innovators, a willingness to reward success and to support failure.
6. A belief in the importance of informality to enhance communication.
7. An explicit belief in the primacy of learning as the objective of the school. (Deal & Kennedy, 1982)

Values are made obvious to the people in an organization by indirect means (Whitaker, McGrevin, & Granier, 1991). Leaders model them, day-to-day practices incorporate them, symbols of the values abound in the organization and the cultural network, the primary but informal communication system carries them throughout the culture (Kouzes & Posner, 1987). As Kouzes and Posner (1987) state, "You cannot lead others until you have first lead yourself through a struggle of opposing values" (p. 302).

The most obvious display of an institution's values is found in who it chooses for its leaders. Cultural linkages include establishing behavioral norms, using symbols, instituting ceremonies, and even telling stories. All of these actions are designed to build the cultural foundations of organizational excellence. We can identify several tasks that involve creating these cultural linkages. These tasks have been identified by analyzing the job of the principal. The list includes:

1. Establishing an atmosphere conducive to learning.
2. Setting high expectations for teachers and students.
3. Setting school-level goals.
4. Instructional leadership—supervising curriculum and teaching.
5. Communicating effectively inside the school.
6. Building parent and community support. (Simpson, 1990)

Effective schools must have effective leaders and such leaders are those who can create and implement a vision of culture that contains, within it, values on which excellence is built. Principals cannot simply be administrators. Effective leaders must be able to create a vision and generate schoolwide support for this vision. Effective school leaders carry out their visions through these actions so that principals can attain the ideal of effective schools (Sashkin, 1988).

Peterson (1988) suggests five ways that leaders reinforce the norms, values, and beliefs in organizational cultures. Cultures are shaped by:

1. What leaders pay attention to, measure, and control.
2. Leader reactions to critical incidents and organizational crisis.
3. Deliberate role-modeling, teaching and coaching by leaders.
4. Criteria for allocation of rewards and status.
5. Criteria for recruitment, selection, promotion, retirement, and communication.

These actions provide incentives for others to act within certain standards.

Hostetler (1986) points out how one fundamental ethical principle, the respect for other persons, can and must be integral to the principal's decision-making process.

Respect for persons requires that principals:

1. Have an active concern for the self-determinancy of others, an appreciation for others' ambitions, feelings, beliefs, etc.
2. Recognize the rule-following aspect of human behavior.
3. Have regard for the intellectual integrity of people.

No amount of caring can make a principal's actions ethical unless care is accompanied by real respect. While respect is a personal relationship in the sense that it exists between persons as persons, it need not be personal in the sense of involving a special sort of attachment or affection. Because we are to respect all people, we must be impersonal to the extent that our special relationships with some people should not always govern our actions toward them.

The vast majority of principals want to do what is right. To do this, they must respect people. They must involve others in the guidance of educational endeavors. This does not require that principals give up their leadership role. Principals need not consult at all times for all things; there are special tasks principals alone should perform. The use of power may be necessary and ethical; but it must be used with respect.

Current management theory appears to reject traditional authoritarian styles in favor of more democratic, participatory approaches. The fact still remains that every managerial style requires that managers exert some sort of influence over others. Influence over others is power.

Sixteen power tactics that describe the power-related behavior of managers and employees have been developed. The power tactics most often used by managers are: ritualism, organizational structure, manipulation of resources, use of rewards, legitimization, use of language and symbols, use of ambiguity, control over agenda preparation, use of objective criteria, use of outside experts, formulation of coalitions, cooptation of opposition, personality, public relations, proactivity and brinksmanship (Fairholm & Fairholm, 1984).

The recent research on power theory, power motives, and power tactics holds promise for the overall effectiveness of school administrators in coping with increasing and decreasing resources as well as a conscious and active work force.

NOTES

Bower, M. (1966). *The will to manage.* New York: McGraw-Hill.

Deal, T.E., & Kennedy, A.A. (1982). *Corporate cultures.* Reading, MA: Addison-Wesley.

Fairholm, G., & Fairholm, B.C. (1984). Sixteen power tactics principals can use to improve management effectiveness. *NASSP Bulletin, 68* (472), 68–74.

Goodlad, J.I. (1984). *A place called school.* New York: McGraw-Hill.

Hostetler, K.S. (1986). Ethics and power: Implications for the principal's leadership. *NASSP Bulletin, 70* (488), 31–36.

Kouzes, T., & Posner, B. (1987). *The leadership challenge.* San Francisco: Jossey-Bass.

Morris, W. (1969). *American Heritage dictionary of the English language.* Boston: Houghton-Mifflin.

Peters, T.J., & Waterman, R.H. (1982). *In search of excellence.* New York: Harper & Row.

Peterson, K.D. (1988). Mechanisms of culture building and principals' work. *Education and Urban Society, 20* (3), 250–261.

Sashkin, M. (1988). The visionary principal. *Education and Urban Society, 20* (3), 239–249.

Simpson, G.H. (1990). Keeping it alive: Elements of school culture that sustain innovation. *Educational Leadership, 47* (8), 34–37.

Webster's New World. (1988). *Webster's New World Dictionary.* Springfield, MA: Merriam-Webster.

Whitaker, K.S., McGrevin, C., & Granier, A. (1991). Know thyself: A prerequisite for educational leaders. *Journal of School Leadership, 1* (2) 168–175.

BIBLIOGRAPHY

330. Anderson, G.L. (1989). *The management of meaning and the achievement of organizational legitimacy: A critical ethnography of the principalship.* (ERIC Document Reproduction Service No. ED 306 663)
Using ethnographic research tools, this study explores the role that the symbolic action of administrators plays in the social construction of reality. Case study data are provided to illustrate meaning management at the school district level. Framing this analysis is the application of the categories of critical theory to the study of educational organizations. Critical theory of organizations involves the three tasks of understanding, critique, and praxis. For the purpose of discussing how meaning was managed, data were gathered from 66 interviews; 28 school board, principal, and central office meeting observations; and the analyses of 30 documents. The goal of the study was to obtain perceptions of selected critical events in order to define the elementary reading program in Fairlawn, an affluent suburban school district. What emerged from the study is that program legitimacy is a scarce resource. It must constantly be won and defined by administrators who are aware of the school's sociocultural constructions, which include its language, rituals, and myths.

331. Davis, D.E. (1984). Should the public schools teach values. *Phi Delta Kappan, 65* (5), 358–360.
Discusses the teaching of values in the public schools. The pros and cons of the recent criticism of secular humanism are addressed. The author suggests there is a need for educators to more effectively address the complex question of teaching values in the school. The task of American educators in public schools is to teach civic, not religious, values.

332. Fairholm, G., & Fairholm, B.C. (1984). Sixteen power tactics principals can use to improve management effectiveness. *NASSP Bulletin, 68* (472), 68–75.
Principals, like most other managers, no longer can influence employees in the way they once did. They still have the authority to issue orders, but they have fewer means of enforcing compliance with those orders. They do not have the reward or punishment potentials of past years.

333.   Fasenmyer, S.A., & Mamana, J. (1984). How to add the human
       dimension for more effective schools. *Tips for Principals from
       NASSP*. (ERIC Document Reproduction Service No. ED 251 960)
       Open communication among administrators, teachers, and students
leads to a more effective learning environment. Teachers who are treated
fairly by administrators will pass this sensitivity and humanity on to
their relationships with students. Administrators can take a number of
steps to establish a communication forum and a school climate that
balances the educational program with a measure of humanity.

334.   Firestone, W.A., & Wilson, B. L. (1984). Culture of school is a
       key to more effective instruction. *NASSP Bulletin, 68* (476), 7–
       11.
       Principals can improve their schools' effectiveness by shaping the
school's culture, and they play an important role in maintaining the
content, symbols, and communication patterns in their schools.

335.   Gezi, K. (1990). The role of leadership in inner-city schools.
       Educational Research Quarterly, 12 (4), 4–11.
       The concept of leadership is defined, and its role in improving
inner-city schools is assessed. Leaders in effective schools and student
motivation are considered. Leaders should reject the cultural deficit notion
and commit themselves to the belief that every child can learn in school
by setting an appropriate pace.

336.   Guth, J., & Williams, R.T. (1984). School administrators—how
       your philosophical orientation affects management practice.
       NASSP Bulletin, 68 (472), 59–67.
       The article attempts to define pragmatism. It looks at pragmatism
from three reference points: (1) the nature of reality; (2) nature of
knowledge; and (3) nature of values. From standpoint number one the
author states that change is the only reality. What man cannot experience
is not real. From standpoint two, truth is revealed and unchanging. From
standpoint three, values are relative.

337.   Hostetler, K.S. (1986). Ethics and power: Implications for the
       principal's leadership. *NASSP Bulletin, 70* (488), 31–36.
       Public concern for educational reform has increased the pressure on
school principals to lead their institutions toward educational excellence.
In the quest for better schools, are we losing track of the ethical side of
leadership?

338. Peterson, K.D. (1988). Mechanisms of culture building and principals' work. *Education and Urban Society, 20* (3), 250–261.
Organizational theory contributes to increased understanding of how schools and school districts work and the challenges to improving and maintaining productivity. One of the key organizational factors is the school principal who, it is hoped, functions as an instructional leader.
This article takes a look at the nature of cultures in schools and illustrates the ways principals may shape and change the culture of schools. It also focuses on the development of school culture with particular attention to the ways principals shape these cultures for effectiveness, productivity, motivation, and commitment of faculties and staff to organizational ends.
This article gives illustrations and provides examples of principals' culture building activities and suggests how those cultures may have influenced schools.

339. Rancifer, J.L. (1990). *How the principal can provide instructional leadership for the reluctant learner.* ERIC Document Reproduction Service No. ED 319 709)
The principal, as an instructional leader of the school, should be certain that each reluctant learner is: (1) provided a school environment where students are rewarded often for their achievements and successes; (2) tangibly rewarded for academic achievement and appropriate behavior; (3) strengthened with strong ties between the home and the school by reaching out to the parents and the community; (4) recognized in assemblies, honor rolls and public lists for achievements; (5) engaged in relevant learning experiences; (6) required to know the expected behavior for achievement in the school; (7) required to do at least 30 minutes of homework per class daily; (8) provided an opportunity to participate in "course help sessions" conducted by teachers; (9) provided an opportunity for a "second chance" test when a test is failed; (10) given the opportunity to be caught doing something good and right; (11) involved in a school activity and some of its planning functions; and (12) provided a program of failure prevention in the first grade.

340. Saphier, J., & King, M. (1985). Good seeds grown in strong cultures. *Educational Leadership, 42* (6), 67–74.
States that the culture of the school is the foundation for school improvement. The authors assert that there are twelve norms of school culture, which include: (1) collegiality, (2) experimentation, (3) high expectations, (4) trust and confidence, (5) tangible support, (6) reaching out to the knowledge bases, (7) appreciation and recognition, (8) caring, celebration, and humor, (9) involvement in decision making, (10)

protection of what's important, (11) traditions, (12) honest, open communication.

341. Sashkin, M. (1988). The visionary principal. *Education and Urban Society, 20* (3), 239–249.

   Principals have a critical role in school improvement. Recent research confirms that students achieve more in schools whose principals are seen as strong leaders.

   The article identified two sets of leadership activities. The first involved creating "bureaucratic linkages," that is, engaging in the managerial and bureaucratic tasks we normally associate with the role of administrator. This means creating and enforcing policies, rules, procedures and authority relations. The second set of activities is less familiar. The aim of the activities in this set is the creation of cultural linkages.

342. Schmuck, P.A. & Schmuck, R.A. (1990). The small-town principal: An endangered species. *Principal, 70* (2), 32–35.

   Describes a study that consisted of interviews with 38 elementary school principals in 21 western and midwestern states. The sample was made up of 27 men and 11 women with an age range of 35 to 64, all of whom worked in small–town schools. The paper describes the various challenges faced by these principals, including academic deficits, children's emotional needs, public demands for higher achievement, decreasing financial resources, and staff improvement needs. Specific case descriptions are offered to illustrate current realities and some exemplary practices for boosting student motivation, teacher improvement, and increasing staff involvement. Some outstanding programs described include: (1) a cooperative approach among administrators, teachers, parents, and students to improve classroom discipline; (2) a home-centered parent education program; (3) low-cost teacher inservice training; (4) teacher peer coaching; and (5) a staff decision-clarification procedure. It is concluded that too many principals continue to work ineffectively in the face of the frustrations to be found in rural schools. A small number of administrators, however, are able to cope successfully with their challenges by using more innovative and democratic approaches to leadership.

343. Stone, F.A. (1986). Intercultural education at high schools in greater Salt Lake City, Utah: An ethnographic inquiry. *Urban Education Reports Series Number Seven.* ERIC Document Reproduction Service No. ED 299 362)

Intercultural education in the greater Salt Lake City (Utah) metropolitan area seems to have minimal effect on high school students' behavior or attitudes. This study was planned in order to better understand the nature and dynamics of intercultural instruction in Salt Lake City. Information was analyzed from the following sources: (1) interviews with local and state educational leaders, observation of community cultural events, and documentary sources; (2) 200 hours of participant observation in public high school classrooms; and (3) a survey of principals of 20 public and seven independent or church related schools. Conclusions included the following: (1) formal instruction was textbook centered, supplemented with some instructional media, and considerable oral interpretation and elaboration by the teacher; (2) students tended to ignore any classroom instruction that would not be later included in examinations, which were textbook centered; (3) minority group students tended to ignore white students at nonformal school-sponsored intercultural events; (4) intercultural instruction at schools operated by the Church of Jesus Christ of Latter Day Saints focused on preparation for missionary roles.

344. Torres, M.E. (1988). Attitudes of bilingual education parents toward language learning and curriculum and instruction. *NABE: The Journal for the National Association for Bilingual Education, 12* (2), 171–185.

An interview survey finds no significant difference in attitudes toward Spanish-English bilingual education between Chicano parents who were members of the bilingual school advisory committee and Chicano parents who were not. Nor were there differences between parents and school principals. Stronger motivation for bilingual education in parents of lower social class children is encouraged.

345. Wimpelberg, R.K. (1986). *Bureaucratic and cultural images in the management of more and less effective schools.* (ERIC Document Reproduction Service No. ED 269 898)

This paper reports on a research study designed, in part, to explore the expression of bureaucracy (or structural management) and culture among principals in Louisiana. In addition, the study compares principals in nine of the schools categorized as "more effective" and nine categorized as "less effective," based on mean scores on the reading section of the Louisiana Basic Skills Test (LBST). Findings disclose an apparent reliance on bureaucratic procedures and externally defined purposes, and a sensitivity to adult (political) influences in the less effective schools. This contrasts with a use of process and symbols, a broad and internally forged definition of purpose, and a "child-as-client" orientation in the more effective schools.

CHAPTER 22

Legal and Regulatory Applications

School principals must have a working knowledge of the legal and regulatory aspects of school operations, including the constitutional considerations, school board/district operations, students' rights and responsibilities, and teachers' rights and responsibilities. Based on the skills needed by school principals as identified by the National Commission for the Principalship (Thomson, 1990, 25), the principal should be prepared to address the following components: (1) acting in accordance with relevant laws, rules and policies; (2) recognizing governmental influences on education; (3) working within local rules, procedures, and directives; and (4) administering contracts.

CHANGES IN LEGAL CONSIDERATIONS

T. van Geel (1988) emphasized the need for understanding the legal and regulatory applications which affect the school administrator. Changes in education as mandated by the courts, starting with the *Brown v. Topeka Board of Education* decision in 1954, to the more recent impact of education reform court decisions concerning funding and the constitutionality of education, have generated a complex demand on the contemporary school leader. Principals must have an awareness of these legal concerns as well as the skills to stay current with new laws from policy, statutes, and court decisions.

Witters-Churchill and Erlandson (1990) stress the importance of having a background or knowledge of legal and regulatory applications. Hoyle, et al. (1990) identified the essential skills of successful school administrators and indicated the importance of understanding the political and legal factors affecting education.

HOW SHOULD PRINCIPALS BE TRAINED?

As state governments decree new reform mandates, school principals must implement the statutes, policies, and regulations. It is the principal who must interpret the intent and impact these mandates have on the local school environment. Preparation of school principals should include the following objectives:

1. Acquiring information on contemporary legal principles as they are applied to the schools.
2. Examining the way courts resolve policy conflicts among students, teachers, administrators, and other community groups.
3. Developing skills used in legal analysis, research, writing, and in the "practice of preventive law."
4. Increasing awareness of the costs and benefits of resolving educational controversies through the legal process and through alternative approaches to conflict resolutions.
5. Identifying topics, practices, policies, regulations required as a knowledge base for state laws and administrators.

EDUCATIONAL LITIGATION

Special emphasis should be given to perspectives which affect public education in a litigious society where people are unafraid to instigate court actions. The most often litigated elements of education are: (1) desegregation and civil rights; (2) religion and the public schools; (3) student admission, control, and rights; (4) personnel issues; and (5) school finance (Knezevich, 1984).

NOTES

Hoyle, J., English, F., & Steffy, B. (1990). *Skills for successful school leaders*. Arlington, VA: American Association of School Administrators.

Knezevich, S.J. (1984). *Administration of public education*. (4th Ed.). New York: Harper & Row.

Thomson, S.D. (1990). *Principals for our changing schools: Preparation and certification*. Fairfax, VA: National Commission for the Principalship.

van Geel, T. (1988). The law and the courts. In N.J. Boyan's *Handbook of research on educational administration*. New York: Longman.

Witters-Churchill, L., & Erlandson, D. A. (1990). *The principalship in the 1990's and beyond: Current research on performance-based preparation and professional development*. Tempe, AZ: The University Council for Educational Administration.

BIBLIOGRAPHY

346. Alexander, K., & Alexander, M.D. (1991). *American public school law*. Third Edition. St. Paul, Minnesota: West Publishing.
Provides a contemporary update on legal principles for educational leaders. The impact of constitutional concerns, operations of school boards, educational reform, student rights, and teachers' rights and responsibilities are identified. The authors have provided a significant update on recent court cases and the impact these decisions have made on education.

347. Bamber, C. (1990). Public school choice: Will we be ready? *Education Digest, 55* (5),19–22.
Emphasizes the changes in school attendance concepts regarding choice. The concepts and current application of public school choice are discussed. The article relates to the legal implications of transfer, arbitrary assignment, and how choice will affect education.

348. Dunklee, D.R. (1990). Site-based management: Implications for risk management? *School Business Affairs, 56* (6), 24–27.
Site-based management opens the possibility of problems in district wide risk management and liability prevention programs. This article describes a program to transfer prevention law and risk management strategies to individual school sites.

349. Fischer, L., Schimmel, D., & Kelly, C. (1987). *Teachers and the law*. (2nd Ed.). New York: Longman.
Relates the legal implications of teachers and educational law. Discussed are teachers' rights and responsibilities and how school administrators must implement policy and regulations to safeguard these principles.

350. Kaplan, L.S., & Geoffrey, K. (1987). The Hatch amendment: A primer for counselors, part 1. *School Counselor, 35* (1), 9–16.
This article reports on the Hatch Amendment which required parental permission before students involved in certain federally funded programs could be psychologically or psychiatrically tested or treated. Describes the development and implementation of the amendment by conservative parent groups and briefly discusses the implications of the act.

351. LaMoret, M. (1990). *School law: Cases and concepts*. New York: Prentice Hall.

Provides a contemporary update on cases and the concepts that affect school law. The impact of court decisions on implementing educational processes concerns the school administrator. Due process and the rights of individuals are given special consideration.

352. Levicoff, S. (1989). Upholding students' religious freedom. *Christian Century, 106* (36), 1108–1109.
The author defends the concept of the Equal Access Law and the principle on which it was based. Arguments for the use of public school facilities by student religious groups are presented. The equal access principle is a key issue with legal implications concerning church/state involvement.

353. Mathis, N. (1989). Oregon students' suit challenges state "safety net." *Education Week, 8* (40), 13.
Offers an insight into how students became involved in a lawsuit against the state of Oregon concerning the school funding provision of the state constitution and the students' equal protection rights. The emphasis of the article relates to a "safety net" provision which was added to stop school closings. The concept relates to many of contemporary reform actions throughout the nation demanding adequate funding for education.

354. Mawdsley, R.D., & Hooker, C.P. (1990). Removal of school board members. *West's Education Law Reporter, 57* (3), 627–44.
Summarizes issues related to removal of school board members, including grounds for dismissal, methods of dismissal, and parties seeking removal. Fewer than 20 successful removal actions have occurred since WWII, which illustrates the difficulty of this action.

355. Menacker, J. (1987). *School law: Theoretical and case perspectives.* New York: Prentice Hall.
Emphasizes the use of case perspectives regarding theory and educational law. The use of case perspectives provides the educator an overview of what may happen when legal theory is applied to the school setting.

356. Rist, M.C. (1990). The threat of litigation has a chilling effect. *Executive Educator, 12* (3), 18.
According to the American Tort Reform Association's (ATRA) survey of secondary school principals, concern about liability was cited as the reason for cutting back or terminating many activities. ATRA recommends some major legislative changes including reform of the

doctrine of joint and several liability, and placing limits on non-economic and punitive damage awards.

357. Rossow, L. F. (1989). *The law of student expulsions and suspensions.* Topeka: National Organization on Legal Problems of Education.

Since the 1975 United States Supreme Court decision of *Goss v. Lopez* the law of expulsion and suspension has reached a high level of complexity. The six sections of this book focus primarily on procedural aspects in the elementary and secondary public school settings involving regular education students. The goal of this book is to help support the school in controlling student behavior while respecting the rights of the student.

358. Rothstein, L. (1990). *Special Education Law.* New York: Longman.

Provides the components necessary for an educator to understand the complexities of school law as it relates to special education. The author gives a good background on the history of special education law and its implications for contemporary education. The details provide a principal the opportunity to be proactive on preventive measures regarding possible legal predicaments regarding special education situations.

359. Salomone, R.C. (1989). Children versus the state: The status of students' constitutional rights. *Proceedings of the Academy of Political Science, 37* (2), 182–200.

Due process and privacy rights of children are the focus of this article. As the constitutional rights of children become a major issue for educators, school leaders must be aware of contemporary concerns on freedom of expression and the due process of students.

360. Stover, D. (1990). The dress mess. *American School Board Journal, 177* (6), 26–29, 33.

Any restrictions on student dress must have a legitimate educational rationale. Standards of attire for school employees are also permissible. A dress code policy that calls for reasonable restrictions and is enforced with common sense can create a better school environment. Restrictive measures can lead to costly lawsuits.

361. Strahan, R.D., & Turner, L.C. (1987). *The courts and the schools.* New York: Longman.

Provides the educator concepts and principles for using preventive measures regarding the legal risks faced as an educator. Emphasizes the school administrator's legal risks of management in a contemporary setting. The fundamentals of school law are identified and described with case law.

362. Thompson, D.C. (1990). School finance and the courts: A reanalysis of progress. *West's Education Law Reporter, 59* (4), 445–61.

Examines federal and state court decisions in school finance litigation involving the argument that education is a fundamental right with equal opportunity and equal protection. Outlines legal strategy for educational reform by arguing that surrogates for these concepts are state education laws requiring uniform and efficient schools.

363. Winter, P.C. (1989). *Regulation of home schooling parents in South Carolina: The state's perspective.* Paper presented at the Annual Meeting of the American Educational Research Association, San Francisco. (ERIC Document Reproduction Service No. ED 306 673)

Includes a discussion of South Carolina's 1988 amendment to the law regulating home schooling instruction. The amendment specifies: (1) procedures for application; (2) instructor qualification; (3) minimum requirements for the instructional program; and (4) physical conditions of the place of instruction.

364. Yell, M.L., & Espin, C.A. (1990). The handicapped children's protection act of 1986: Time to pay the piper? *Exceptional Children, 56*, (5), 396–407.

Provides the key identifying factors for the provision of appropriate educational opportunities for handicapped children. The success of special education and these educational opportunities is based on the ability of the parents to use the due process mechanisms of the act to resolve disputes between the parents and the schools. The law, Education for all Handicapped Children Act, is discussed, including implications for administrators.

365. Yudof, M.G., Kirp, D.L., & Levin, B. (1992) *Educational policy and the law.* (3rd Ed.). St. Paul, MN: West.

This new edition of a standard treatise on educational law stresses the relationship between law and policy. The book also addresses legal decisions as compared to educational practice. The book uses a variety of sources, not just law cases. It offers perspectives to the principal on both the political and policy concerns in legal issues.

366.   Zirkel, P.A. (1989). A chilling effect on evaluation? *Phi Delta Kappan, 71* (2), 164–165.

Presents the arguments concerning the use of teacher evaluation and the ramifications it has for educators, particularly principals. The author provides references and concepts related to the effective use of teacher evaluation and possible abuse. The importance of effective policy and procedures used for teacher evaluation are discussed.

367.   Zirkel, P.A. (1991, April). End of story. *Phi Delta Kappan, 72* (8), 640–641.

In reviewing court decisions which are reported, the entire story of a case may not always be presented. This concept is true in regard to cases of reversals by an appellate court. The article provides the example of a court case involving parents' rights of privacy and students' freedom from involuntary servitude.

368.   Zirkel, P.A., & Richardson, S. (1988). *A digest of supreme court decisions affecting education.* Bloomington, IN: Phi Delta Kappa.

Offers the educator an overview of the major court decisions which currently affect education. Issues covered are church/state relations, school finance and reform, rights and responsibilities, civil rights, and procedural parameters.

CHAPTER 23
Policy and Political Influences

Education is a political process. Education is a public institution created by and for the people. As such, rules and regulations are necessary to a representative form of government. Politics are concerned with the distribution and limitation of decision-making power while "policy is the statement of an official decision that guides the making of other decisions" (Orlosky, et al., 1984).

WHO MAKES POLICY?

The United States Constitution specified that any power not specifically accorded the federal government was reserved for the state. Consequently, education has been interpreted as a state function (Brademas, 1987). State legislature and governors have been very active in the past decade establishing education policy and programs. Most states grant local boards of education policy making authority under the broad guidelines established by the state legislature (Rourke, 1976). Hawaii is a notable exception to this rule because they have only one school system.

Local school boards typically make policy for individual school districts. Policy making is a public responsibility that should be considered seriously by all involved in making educational decisions. School boards should consider seriously policy statements and policy positions and how such policy will impact schools and students. Administrators, principals, teachers, and communities should have the opportunity to have input into policy deliberations. Principals should take every opportunity to impact policy decisions.

WHAT IS THE PURPOSE OF POLICY?

Educational policy is necessary to give direction and accountability to educational organizations. Policy decisions made by local boards of education have the impact of law. Policy is the official or "company line" on an issue. According to Lindblom and Braybrooke (1963), changes in public policy tend to be "incremental." Policy makers are often uncomfortable with broad, sweeping changes and innovation that may disturb the status quo. Downs (1967) goes on to postulate that the "vast majority of [policy-makers] . . . become conservers in the long run" (p. 16). According to Rourke (1976), policy making has been structured "by two not always consistent objectives—responsiveness and effectiveness" (p. 143).

WHO IMPACTS POLICY DECISIONS?

Policy decisions should be held in open forum and be accessible to the public. In recent years, more special interest groups have attempted to impact educational policy. Historically, boards of education relied on administrators (primarily superintendents), parent-teacher groups, and citizen advisory committees for input (Bennett, 1985). However, as a more diverse constituency attempted to avail themselves of educational services, more specialized interest groups presented their views to boards of education.

LEVELS OF EDUCATIONAL POLICY

Educational policy decisions are made at three levels: state, district, and local school. State boards of education often interpret the laws passed by the state legislature as state rules and regulations (Shapiro, 1982). Administrative interpretations of rules and regulations also carry the impact of law (Smith, 1983).

Local boards of education make policy decisions which superintendents interpret as administrative policy. In addition, local schools often make policy decisions, particularly in shared governance schools. In the absence of some form of participatory management, principals make school policy. Teachers also make policy decisions about what takes place in their classrooms (Ball, 1987).

POLITICAL CLIMATE OF EDUCATIONAL ADMINISTRATION

Principals are often caught in the middle of school-community or intracommunity conflicts. Principals must be aware of the external power sources in the community. Who are the king-makers or power brokers in the community (Lasswell, 1936)? Without this knowledge, principals may find themselves in untenable positions.

In addition to external community politics, internal political concerns within the school district and the schools present problems for principals. Competition for power, prestige, or scarce resources is part of the local political area (Gronn, 1983). System-wide struggles for promotion and finances can place the principal in the position of fighting a mentor (superintendent) for resources at the request of a constituency (teachers) that do not appreciate the principal's precarious position (Knezevich, 1984).

NOTES

Ball, S.J. (1987). *The micro-politics of the school.* London: Routledge.

Bennett, N. (1985). Central control and parental influence: Reconciling the tensions in current proposals for school governance and policy making. *Educational Management and Administration, 12* (3), 157–163.

Brademas, J. (1987). *The politics of education: Conflict and consensus on Capitol Hill.* Norman, OK: University of Oklahoma Press.

Downs, A. (1967). *Inside bureaucracy.* Boston: Little, Brown and Company.

Gronn, P. (1983). Talk as work: The accomplishment of school administration. *Administrative Science Quarterly, 28,* 1–21.

Knezevich, S.J. (1984). *Administration of public education.* (4th Ed.). New York: Harper and Row.

Lasswell, H. (1936). *Politics: Who gets what, when, how.* New York: Whittlesey.

Lindblom, C.E., & Braybrooke, D. (1963). *A strategy of decision.* New York: Free Press.

Orlosky, D.E., McCleary, L.E., Shapiro, A., & Webb, L.D. (1984). *Educational Administration Today.* New York: Merrill.

Rourke, F.E. (1976). *Bureaucracy, politics, and public policy.* (2nd Ed.). Boston: Little, Brown and Company.

Shapiro, H.S. (1982). Education in capitalist society: Towards a reconstruction of the state in educational policy. *Teachers College Record, 82* (4), 515–525.

Smith, T.J. (1983). On being political. *Educational Management and Administration, 11,* 205–208.

Wiles, D.K., Wiles, J., & Bondi, J. (1981). *Practical politics for school administrators.* Boston: Allyn and Bacon.

BIBLIOGRAPHY

369. *Restructuring education in North Carolina: A synthesis of eight education reform reports.* (1991). (ERIC Document Reproduction Service No. ED 333 551)
Eight reports have been released that deal with restructuring education in North Carolina. Although the reports differ, two themes predominate: (1) there should be high expectations of all students, accompanied by a strengthened curriculum; and (2) there should be a focus on student outcomes as a means of evaluating the state's educational system and becoming accountable to the public. Other themes include decentralized decision making, closer school-business-parent partnerships, and increased investment in staff through better salaries and training. Changes in certification standards and changes in school finance designed to ensure a basic education for every child are the policy recommendations contained in the reports.

370. Boysen, T.C. (1990) Irreconcilable differences? Effective schools vs. restructuring. *California School Boards Journal, 49* (2), 66–67, 69–73.
Small- and medium-sized school systems have been the most successful in implementing the effective schools movement. Confronting the necessities of poor and minority students has forced urban school districts to explore restructuring options. The effective schools model should be incorporated into restructuring. School effectiveness strengths need to be incorporated into restructuring models.

371. Deal, T.E., & Peterson, K.D. (1990). The principal's role in shaping school culture. (ERIC Document Reproduction Service No. ED 325 914)
Principals can shape school culture. Current pressures for school reform are described: (1) the human resources approach; (2) the structural model; (3) the political model; (4) the free market model; and (5) the school culture model. The book describes organizational cultures and presents evidence connecting organizational culture to productivity in schools. The principal shapes a school culture by fulfilling five roles: (1) symbol, (2) potter, (3) poet, (4) actor, and (5) healer. Successful principal tactics are reported: (1) identify what is important; (2) select compatible teachers; (3) deal successfully with conflict; (4) set a consistent example; (5) tell illustrative stories; and (6) use ceremonies, tradition, rituals, and symbols to display the school's common values. Principals must have a desire and commitment to build cultures that support and create excellence.

372. Hanson, M. (1991). *Alteration of influence relations in school-based management.* (ERIC Document Reproduction Service No. ED 332 352)

The influence of school-based management on a district office and schools and between principals and teachers is examined in this report. Five innovative initiatives implemented in the Dade County Public Schools—peer evaluation, different teacher roles, block scheduling, school-within-a-school, and teachers as advisors—were evaluated. School level discretion was allowed in some areas of decision-making, most deviations from regular policy were subject to approval by central office administrators. Teacher involvement altered teacher-principal relations, which were mitigated by principal supervision of the innovation and limited teacher involvement. The pilot school-based management project recorded no change in district/school relations.

373. Johnson, T.P. (1990). *Procedural due process and fairness in student discipline. A legal memorandum.* (ERIC Document Reproduction Service No. ED 315 888)

The Supreme Court decided that the Constitution requires public school principals to follow procedural due process in suspension and expulsion cases. Constitutional due process required when public school officials are investigating allegations of student misconduct and determining disciplinary sanctions are examined. The following topics are discussed: (1) codes and student conduct; (2) constitutional due process and fundamental fairness; (3) constitutional due process for long-term suspensions and expulsions; and (4) suspension or expulsion of handicapped students.

374. Kshensky, M., & Muth, R. (1991). *The mutual empowerment of teachers and principals.* (ERIC Document Reproduction Service No. ED 332 377)

This article begins with a review of traditional perspectives on educational leadership including the link between effective principals and school effectiveness, and the bases of social power. This document reports on a study to determine how the types of power used by principals relate to school effectiveness. Relationships between power behaviors, school effectiveness, and the mutual empowerment of teachers and principals are described. Principal power behaviors elicit different responses from their teachers. The use of influence is the principal power most conducive to mutual empowerment, positive organizational climate, and improved teacher performance.

375. La Raus, R. (1989). Business and the education revolution. *Councilor, 49*, 6–9.

Provides an overview of the influence United States business has had on education reform. Several post-1975 expectations for education are identified, including the changing role of the school principal.

376. Murphy, J. (1990). A response to "Agenda for reform: A critical appraisal." *Journal of Education Policy, 5* (2), 193.

This article concerns the author's critique of the National Policy Board for Educational Administration's agenda for reforming administrator education. Practitioner viewpoints are represented as well as information from other professional organizations. The National Policy Board proposed a new policy for administrator preparation.

377. Passow, A.H. (1984). *Reforming schools in the 1980s. A critical review of the national reports. Urban Diversity Series, Number 87.* (ERIC Document Reproduction Service No. ED 242 859)

A plethora of reform reports were published in the early 1982. The historical context of the reports is based on a discussion of secondary education and reform proposals since the 19th century. This paper examines the relationship of excellence to equity.

378. Rallis, S.F. (1990). *The classroom alternative process: School change policy into practice.* (ERIC Document Reproduction Service No. ED 332 277)

This article describes a program designed to reduce student referrals to special education programs. This study evaluates the program together with its impact on classroom teacher policy. The findings indicate that the program contributed to an overall change in teachers' problem-solving practices as well as to a reduction in student referrals. The authors speculate that the program succeeded because of teacher specificity, adaptability, recognition of cognitive and organizational structures, and provision for actual change.

379. Rosario, J.R. (1990). Guiding principles are not enough: On thinking, folly, and middle school reform. *Journal of Education Policy, 50* (3), 273–281.

Educational change literature suggests that good intentions and noble visions are not sufficient to accomplish educational reform. This report examines one principal's frustrated attempts to reform a middle school using guidelines from "Turning Points." Change is shown to be a policy issue which often becomes political.

380. Sergiovanni, T.J. (1991). Constructing and changing theories of practice: The key to preparing school administrators. *Urban Review, 23* (1), 39–49.

The author discusses methods for preparing school administrators to be more reflective of the moral implications of their practice. The link between theory and practice should be more informed and deliberate.

381. Short, P.M., & Greer, J.T. (1989). *Increasing teacher autonomy through shared governance: Effects on policy making and student outcomes.* (ERIC Document Reproduction Service No. ED 319 096)

Shared governance permits an increase in teacher autonomy and contributes to their role in determining school policy. This paper describes the policy impact of shared governance in nine autonomous schools where the participants at each site have provided some insight into policy issues. The project helps principals to reconceptualize their roles from directors of their schools to developers of human potential; to aid teachers in decision making and in taking decision-making responsibility. If participative decision making is to be successfully implemented, a wide range of policy changes will need to occur, including a reframing of the traditional roles of administrators and teachers within a given building, the placement of decision-making authorities within the school building and district, and the involvement of school constituencies in all aspects of school life.

382. Stevenson, Z., Jr., & Chunn, E.W. (1991). *Uniform policy/dress codes: School staff and parent perceptions of need and impact.* (ERIC Document Reproduction Service No. ED 331 933)

This study examines the impact of uniform/dress codes and parent perceptions of policy. Findings indicate that parents are more receptive to changing policy when the need is apparent and impact is minimal.

CHAPTER 24

Public and Media Relations

Effective communication between the school/school district and the community is vital to the success of education. Not only should educators understand the community members and implement programs which meet student and community needs, but the community is the greatest source of support for school programs (Orlosky, 1984).

WHAT IS PUBLIC RELATIONS?

Grunig and Hunt (1984) define public relations as the "management of communication between an organization and its publics" (p. 11), in this case, between a school and its community. The National Public Relations Association (1984) states that "educational public relations is a planned systematic management function designed to improve the programs and services of an educational organization" (p. 3). An effective public relations program has the following characteristics: (1) planned; (2) systematic or continuous; (3) listening and responding; (4) strategy development; (5) internal and external; (6) open and honest; (7) essential to management; (8) involves issues management; and (9) personal communication (Bogin, Ferguson, & Mary, 1985).

WHO IS RESPONSIBLE FOR PUBLIC RELATIONS?

Several individuals may be responsible for public relations in a school district: a public relations specialist, the superintendent, or principals. All have a role to play.

THE PRINCIPAL'S ROLE

Principals are primarily responsible for public relations in their schools. A principal can use many communications strategies to "get the message out." Newsletters, surveys, parent-teacher conferences and advisory groups can both be effective at the school level. Principals should not overlook the contributions of teachers, staff, and students when implementing the public relations strategies.

PLANNING FOR PUBLIC RELATIONS

Bogin, et al. (1985) state that school public relations can be handled in a four step process: (1) research, (2) plan, (3) communicate, and (4) evaluate. Although these steps sound like common sense or standard operations procedure, the steps should be internalized by the principal until they become automatic.

WORKING WITH THE MEDIA

Communication with the public is equally important as good interschool communication. Planning the public relations program, attending to informal messages, fostering two-way communications, handling the media, and conducting opinion surveys are all important factors in working with either parents or the media.

CRISIS COMMUNICATION

The school principal is often in the vanguard when a crisis occurs. Whether the crisis is caused by nature or man-made, the media will always be present. School safety concerns can also be media events. School science laboratory safety has been a topic of media concern in recent months (Gentry & Richardson, 1991).

PUBLIC RELATIONS: EVERYONE'S CONCERN

Good public relations is the responsibility of everyone from the custodian to the chair of the school board. Everyone has a role in promoting public confidence in schools. Given the current educational environment, principals must play the key role in acquainting all staff members about their role and their responsibility and also evaluating the school public relations program to determine effectiveness.

HOW TO

West (1985) specifies the following functions of a [principal] in establishing a good public relations program.

1) Radiate confidence.
2) Evince expertise and honesty.
3) Demonstrate product conviction.
4) Dress with decorum.
5) Walk, talk, and listen with purpose and care.
6) Be affirmative and mannerly.
7) Consider students as clients.
8) Display interest in others.
9) Avoid gossip and rumors.
10) Encourage participation (p. 32–35).

NOTES

Bogin, D., Ferguson, D., & Marx, G. (1985). *Public relations for administrators.* Arlington, VA: American Association of School Administrators.

Gentry, L.R., & Richardson, M.D. (1991). Principals—Are your science labs safe? *NASSP Bulletin, 75* (534), 90–94.

Grunig, J.E., & Hunt, T. (1984). *Managing public relations.* New York: Holt, Rinehart and Winston.

National School Public Relations Association. (1984). *Evaluating your school public relations investment.* Arlington, VA: NSPRA.

Orlosky, D.E., McCleary, L.E., Shapiro, A., & Webb, L.D. (1984). *Educational administration today.* New York: Merrill.

West, P.T. (1985). *Educational public relations.* Beverly Hills, CA: Sage.

BIBLIOGRAPHY

383. Ascough, L. (1986). Managing the school PR effort: Not an impossible task. *NASSP Bulletin, 70* (494), 14, 16–18.

Principals are responsible for the public relations effort in their schools, although they often face time constraints and lack of formal training. This article provides a checklist for building a successful campaign, including polling staff talents, reaching out to the community, obtaining district assistance, and making the right approach. Principals are in the best position to carry out the school's public relations program.

384. Au Pawlas, G., & Myers, K. (1989). The principal and communication. *Elementary Principal Series No. 3.*

The third of six volumes in the "elementary principal series," this booklet is intended for beginning elementary principals desiring to develop an effective communications plan for reaching their various publics. The principal plays a key role in controlling both the quantity and quality of school communications. Although principals may feel more comfortable using one-way communication methods (newsletters, bulletins, and media announcements), they should also employ survey questionnaires, conferences, and other means to obtain feedback. Effective school communication plans are continuous, open, and frequent and involve staff and students. Elements characterizing healthy communications with staff include honesty, attentiveness, clarity, and consistency. The tone used in written or oral communications should reflect purpose and desired outcome. The principal must use every available avenue to communicate positive messages about the school tailored to different constituencies. Various communication methods (speaking engagements, newspaper and television coverage, and school newsletters), carry certain advantages and disadvantages. Telephone calls (both positive and problem) and conferences can be effective, if used appropriately. Tips are provided for communicating with peers and the central office.

385. Brock, M.L. (1982). The principal and public relations. *Momentum, 13* (3), 15–17.

The school principal is the most effective public relations vehicle of the school. Principals are encouraged to be visible, improve the school's image in the community, and establish a professional presence. Both verbal and nonverbal communication are critical to influencing public perceptions. Principals should learn to control their powers of perception.

386. Corbett, W.D. (1989). Let's tell the good news about reading and writing. *Educational Leadership, 46* (7), 53.

Principals should highlight elementary school children's reading and writing accomplishments. Principals can hear students read aloud in the hallway, send interesting compositions to the superintendent's office, and post creative writing efforts on the walls of local banks, pizza parlors, and district conference rooms. These activities are needed because the media will seldom report good news about education.

387. Criscuolo, N.P. (1985). A little PR goes a long way. *Principal, 64* (3), 33–34.

Several techniques are suggested that principals can employ to increase positive media coverage. Public knowledge of local educational developments are critical to a school's success.

388. Foley, C.F. (1986). Dealing with crises: One principal's experience. *NASSP Bulletin, 70* (494), 46–51.

The principal of Concord High School (New Hampshire) recounts four crises from the 1984–1985 school year—visits by teacher-astronaut Christa McAuliffe and Secretary of Education William Bennett, the shooting of a former student, and the Challenger Space Shuttle explosion. All took place during one school year. Resuming the normal schedule and fielding media pressures were the two greatest challenges faced by the principal.

389. Gorton, R.A. (1984). An administrator-reporter conflict. *Journal of Educational Public Relations, 7* (1), 8–10.

This article is a two-part scenario concerning a principal's failed attempt to convince a reporter to do a "good news" story about his school. A damaging story later is written by the reporter about the principal's unwillingness to disclose details of an event that might reflect badly on the school. Conflict is often inevitable but both principal and reporter must understand the role and function of the other.

390. Greenbaum, S., et al. (1986). *Educated public relations: School safety 101. With engineering consent.* Sacramento, CA: Safety Council.

This book is designed to enable school administrators to actively participate in planning and implementing school safety and public relations activities. It provides a conceptual framework of the public school relations process and shows its practical application to the problems of school crime and student misbehavior, through discussion of school public relations strategies and tactics to promote safe schools.

391. Jay, B. (1989). Managing a crisis in the school—tips for principals. *NASSP Bulletin, 73* (513), 14, 16–18.

A crisis can happen at any school—even award-winning schools in good neighborhoods. Whether it's due to Mother Nature or to human nature, the media arrive within minutes to record a crisis. This article provides a case-study format to describe recommendations for principals on how to handle a school crisis.

392. Long, C. (1985). How to get community support. *Principal, 64* (5), 28–30.

Principals known for their successful community support programs were surveyed to determine their effective techniques. Their methods were categorized as: (1) effective written and oral communications; (2) community involvement in decision making; (3) use of school volunteers; and (4) encouragement of parent-faculty organizations.

393. Ordovensky, P. (1986). Dealing with the media: Honesty is the best policy. *NASSP Bulletin, 70* (494), 35–37.

Using an English teacher as an example, this article shows that a good public relations program can be built without formally trained PR professionals. The principal can conduct an effective program by initiating friendly relationships with local reporters, facilitating two-way communication, and being honest when asked tough questions.

394. Pfeiffer, I. & Bennett, P. (1988). The principal and the media program. *Clearing House, 62* (4), 183–185.

The (1) tasks of media specialists; (2) standards of the state board of education and of accrediting agencies; and (3) media specialists' responsibilities in planning media programs, public relations efforts, and other media activities are examined from the principal's perspective. Recommendations for using the principal's knowledge of the community is important to the media specialist.

395. Pulling, J. (1989). We can learn from business—And teach a thing or two. *Executive Educator, 11* (4), 32–33.

A collaborative arrangement between education and business can have benefits for both. Schools can learn about fiscal accountability, empowering subordinates, and corporate culture from businesses. Business leaders can learn from school leaders about how people acquire knowledge, professional development, and remotivating the unproductive employee.

396. Richardson, D.M. (1988). *Improving communication with elementary school parents through a targeted communications program involving classroom teachers and the principal.* (ERIC Document Reproduction Service No. ED 302 338)

An elementary school principal implemented a program to improve school-home communication at a school where administrators believed that poor communication between parents and teachers negatively influenced the school's academic and parent involvement programs. The program focused on developing processes that would improve school-home communication. Both written communication and personal approaches were used. The initial findings indicate the program was successful.

397. Shaw, R.C. (1987). Advice for principals: Do's and don'ts for dealing with the press. *NASSP Bulletin, 71* (503), 99–102.

Principals must, on occasion, deal with the news media. This article lists several do's and don'ts which will make the principals' job more effective and less stressful.

398. Zelling, G.L. (1990). Linking schools and social services: The case of child abuse reporting. *Educational evaluation and policy analysis, 12* (1), 41–55.

Public school principals were surveyed to determine coordination of schools and child protective services concerning child abuse reporting. National data reveal that school staffs generally comply with reporting laws. Policies limiting reports and focusing resources on the most serious cases should be addressed.

SECTION SIX
PROJECTIONS

CHAPTER 25

Summary, Conclusions, and Recommendations

SUMMARY

Change is inevitable. How people respond to that change, however, varies, and this response is often a determining factor in the ultimate acceptance or rejection of that change.

A small boy asked a wise, old man, "Where does change really come from?" Hoping to assist the boy, he answered, "From within." That was a good answer. But when further prodded by the boy, "What is necessary for change to occur from within?" The old man rethought his answer and replied, "Exposure to new ideas through education."

CONCLUSIONS

There are five major areas in which change is taking place regarding the role of the school administrator.

1) There is an extensive redesigning of formal principal preparation programs which will focus more on application and less on theory.

2) There is an increased concern for providing informal, continuing principal training programs through the school districts, either by way of inservice or professional development.

3) School reform efforts are having a tremendous impact on both the person, the principal, and the position, the principalship.

4) The changing demographics of the principalship, i.e. retirements, ethnicity, gender, age, etc. will significantly affect the principalship.

5) Due to the above, the changing role of the principal is having a direct effect on all others at the school.

As stated in the introduction, the expectations prior to reviewing the literature were that changes would be found in the *role* itself. However, changes were found in the *role*, the *person*, and the *position*. Sadly, some principals are conducting business in much the same way as their predecessors in the early 1900s.

However, the old ways are simply unacceptable today. The closed-minded bureaucratic attitudes from yesterday have become less effective and more damaging to the members of the staff, faculty, students, parents, and principals themselves. Change is inevitable, but change is an individual thing. No *one* can force *another* to change. The impetus for change can be external, but the rationale for change is internal. Until the need for change is internalized by principals, educational reform is rhetoric without substance.

Change in public school administration practices, due partly to the change in administration preparation programs, is a process, not an event. Change is a journey, not a destination. It is essential that administrators be exposed to new and better ideas to enable them to realize the importance of changing themselves. How does change happen? One principal, one school at a time.

RECOMMENDATIONS

The following recommendations are a reflection of the material collected and assimilated in this book:

To principals:

1) *Learn through self direction.*

    Preparation programs can start the learning process, but principals must continually be learners on the job.

2) *Capitalize on prior experience.*

    Learn from the mistakes of others; a person cannot live long enough to make every mistake. Share with each other; there is no sense in continuing to "reinvent the wheel."

3) *Engage in critical and reflective thinking.*

Reflective thinking provides a great opportunity for problem analysis. Do not overlook the chance to learn from reflection of personal experiences.

To school districts:

1) *Capitalize on peer problem-solving activities.*
   Provide opportunity for principals to learn from each other. Do not hide all the talent in one school or one segment of the district, rather share problems and solutions.

2) *Provide continuous staff development.*
   Staff development opportunities should be available to all principals. As reform changes education, principal skills constantly must be polished. Principals can acquire new skills through input-practice-application cycles.

To universities:

1) *The curriculum for principal preparation programs should be theory-based and practice driven.*
   Preparation programs should mesh content with practice, not one at the exclusion of the other. Such programs should continually change to meet the needs of current and future principals. Problem-based learning is an appropriate instructional strategy.

2) *The learner should be seen as a source of expert knowledge.*
   Preparation programs must abandon the "cookbook" mentality and prepare principals to be creative thinkers and risk-taking leaders.

Index

SOURCE BOOKS ON EDUCATION

1. Bilingual Education: *A Source Book for Educators*, by Alba N. Ambert and Sarah Melendez
2. Reading and Study Skills in the Secondary Schools: *A Source Book*, by Joyce N. French
3. Creating Connections: *Books, Kits, and Games for Children*, by Betty P. Cleaver, Barbara Chatton, and Shirley Vittum Morrison
4. Gifted, Talented, and Creative Young People: *A Guide to Theory, Teaching, and Research*, by Morris I. Stein
5. Teaching Science to Young Children: *A Resource Book*, by Mary D. Iatridis
6. Microcomputers and Social Studies: *A Resource Guide for the Middle and Secondary Grades*, by Joseph A. Braun, Jr.
7. Special Education: *A Source Book*, by Manny Sternlicht
8. Computers in the Classroom . . . What Shall I Do?: *A Guide*, by Walter Burke
9. Learning to Read and Write: The Role of Language Acquisition and Aesthetic Development, *A Resource Guide*, by Ellen J. Brooks
10. School Play: *A Source Book*, by James H. Block and Nancy R. King
11. Computer Simulations: *A Source Book to Learning in an Electronic Environment*, by Jerry Willis, Larry Hovey, and Kathleen Hovey
12. Day Care: *A Source Book*, by Kathleen Pullan Watkins and Lucius Durant, Jr.
13. Project Head Start: *Past, Present, and Future Trends in the Context of Family Needs*, by Valora Washington and Ura Jean Oyemade
14. Adult Literacy: *A Source Book and Guide*, by Joyce French
15. Mathematics Education in Secondary Schools and Two-Year Colleges: *A Source Book*, by Louise S. Grinstein and Paul J. Campbell
16. Black Children and American Institutions: *An Ecological Review and Resource Guide*, by Valora Washington and Velma LaPoint
17. Resources for Educational Equity: *A Source Book for Grades Pre-Kindergarten–12*, by Merle Froschl and Barbara Sprung
18. Multicultural Education: *A Source Book*, by Patricia G. Ramsey, Edwina Battle Vold, and Leslie R. Williams
19. Sexuality Education: *A Resource Book*, by Carol Cassell and Pamela M. Wilson
20. Reforming Teacher Education: *Issues and New Directions*, edited by Joseph A. Braun, Jr.
21. Educational Technology: *Planning and Resource Guide Supporting Curriculum*, by James E. Eisele and Mary Ellin Eisele
22. Critical Issues in Foreign Language Instruction, edited by Ellen S. Silber
23. The Education of Women in the United States: *A Guide to Theory, Teaching, and Research*, by Averil Evans McClelland
24. Materials and Strategies for the Education of Trainable Mentally Retarded Learners, by James P. White
25. Rural Education: *Issues and Practice*, by Alan J. DeYoung
26. Educational Testing. *Issues and Applications*, by Kathy E. Green
27. The Writing Center: *New Directions*, edited by Ray Wallace and Jeanne Simpson
28. Teaching Thinking Skills: *Theory and Practice*, by Joyce N. French and Carol Rhoder